THE
HISTORY
OF THE
VESTAL VIRGINS
OF ROME

(1934)

The best book anywhere on this subject! Contents: Religious Duties; The Sacred Fire; Drowning of the Dummies; Festival of Vesta; Civil Duties, Privileges, Dress, and Discipline of the Vestals; The Vestals During the Empire; The Abolition of the Order; Virgins of the Sun among the Incas of Peru; Hestia of Greece; Topography of Ancient Buildings, Streets, and Monuments connected with the Cult; The End of the Vestals; The Shrine of Mercury; plus much more! Illustrated.

T. Cato Worsfold

ISBN 0-7661-0094-4

Kessinger Publishing, LLC

U.S.A.

http://www.kessingerpub.com

The History of the Vestal Virgins of Rome

by

SIR T. CATO WORSFOLD, BT.

M.A., LL.D., ETC.

AUTHOR OF "THE FRENCH STONEHENGE," BEING AN ACCOUNT
OF THE PRINCIPAL MEGALITHIC REMAINS IN THE MORBIHAN
ARCHIPELAGO, "STAPLE INN AND ITS STORY," "THE SERPENT
COLUMN OF THE DELPHIC ORACLE," ETC.

(Second Impression, revised and enlarged)

London : Rider & Co.
Paternoster House, E.C.

THE HIGH VESTAL FLAVIA PUBLICIA (A.D. 257)

"Nihil apud Romanos Templo Vestae sanctius habetur."

"Among the Romans nothing is held more holy than the Temple of Vesta" (St. AUGUSTINE, *De Civitate Dei*, III, 28).

Made and Printed in Great Britain at
The Mayflower Press, Plymouth. William Brendon & Son, Ltd.
1934

LIST OF AUTHORS QUOTED AND CONSULTED

A
Ambrose.
Ammianus Marcellinus.
Antistius Labeo.
Appian.
Apollodorus.
Apuleius.
Asconius.
Augustine (St.).
Aulus Gellius.
Aurelius Victor.

B
Baker (G. P.)
Bell (W. G.).

C
Capitolinus.
Catullus.
Cicero.
Clark (A.).
Claudian.

D
Diodorus Siculus.
Dion Cassius.
Dionysius of Halicarnassus.

E
Eutropius.

F
Fabius Pictor.
Farnell.
Festus Valerius.
Florus.
Forbes, Russell.
Frazer, Sir James.
Furneaux.

G
Gallianus.
Giraldus Cambrensis.
Gordianus.
Gruter.

H
Hemelario.
Herodian.
Holland, Philemon.
Horace.

J
Josephus.
Julius Obsequens.
Juvenal.

L
Lactantius.
Lampridius.
Langhorne (translator).
Laurentius.
Lefevre, André.
Ligorius.
Livy.
Lucan.
Lucius Faunus.

M
Macrobius.
Martial.
Mommsen.
More (Sir Thomas).

O
Orrery (Earl of).
Ovid.

5

P

Panvinio.
Pauly.
Pliny.
Plutarch.
Prescott.
Procopius (A.D. 550).
Propertius.
Prudentius.
Pusey.
Preller.

R

Rose.

S

Sallust.
Seneca.
Servius.
Solinus.
Spartianus.
Suetonius.
Symmachus.

T

Tacitus.
Teubner (Tr.).
Theodoret.
Theodosius.
Tiberius.
Trebellius Pollio.

V

Valerius Maximus.
Varro.
Vergil.
Vopiscus.

W

Warde Fowler.
Wissowa (Georg).

Z

Zosimus.

CONTENTS

PART I

PART II

CONTENTS

LIST OF ILLUSTRATIONS

INTRODUCTION

AS far back as it is possible to trace the old religions of mankind, and in cases where primitive religions are still to be observed in savage countries, one finds as a feature of many cults, in various ages and countries, establishments of Virgin Priestesses, or religious votaries as an important adjunct to the worship of the Deity.

Of these establishments, perhaps the best known is that of the Vestal Virgins of Rome.

As I know of no exhaustive account of the Vestals in the English language, I have sought in these pages to trace the history of the foundation from its beginning (715 B.C.) to its extinction under Theodosius in A.D. 394, to set forth the status, functions and privileges of its members during this period of over one thousand years ; to describe and discuss the temples served and hostels occupied by the Vestals, both as recorded in Latin and Greek authors and as shown by their existing remains ; and finally, to give some account of similar foundations in other countries and other ages.

In modern days the sisterhoods of the nuns of the Church of Rome, themselves of great antiquity, offer the closest resemblance.

In carrying out this work I have endeavoured as far as possible to let the ancient writers tell the story in their own words, and in order that it may appeal to a wider circle of readers, I have given statements of those writers in English, using accepted and standard translations where such exist, and where there is no translation of this kind, offering an original version.

As, however, no translation is wholly satisfactory, I

have also given extracts from the originals in the text of my book, when the extracts are short enough to be included there, or in an appendix, when the passages quoted are too long to make such a method convenient, and might therefore mar the continuity of the narrative.

T. CATO WORSFOLD.

September, 1932

A second impression being required, I have taken the opportunity to make therein certain desirable revisions and additions.

T. CATO WORSFOLD.

January, 1934.

PART I

ORIGIN AND EARLIER HISTORY OF THE FOUNDATION

(THE WORSHIP OF VESTA)

THE origin of the Vestal Virgins as an organised cult, in Rome, may be said to date from the time of Numa Pompilius (B.C. 715), a Sabine and second King of Rome.

Its beginnings, however, are far earlier and are indeed lost in the mists of antiquity, although we speak of Numa, the High Priest-King, as the founder of the order, since our records commence here. There were Vestals at Tibur (*Corpus Inscriptionum Latinarum*, XIV, Nos. 3677, 3679), and there was also a very ancient worship of Vesta at Lavinium, the city named after Amata's daughter Lavinia, the ancestress of the Alban Kings. The earliest Vestals whom we find mentioned in connection with Roman History are Rhea Silvia, the mother of Romulus, and Tarpeia who betrayed the Citadel to the Sabines.

Both these, however, were Vestals of Alba Longa, not of Rome. At Lavinium, the Roman Consuls, Prætors, and Dictators had to sacrifice to Vesta when they entered upon or laid down their office. (Servius on Vergil, *Æneid*, II, l. 296 ; Macrobius, *Saturn.* ; III, 4, 11.)

At Rome two brothers, Numitor and Amulius, were rivals for the throne. Amulius drove out his elder brother, and appointed the latter's daughter, Rhea Silvia, as a vestal, pretending to do her honour but really to prevent her having children. (Livy, I, 3.)

The name Vesta is cognate with Hestia, softened by the Latins to Vesta, who was the daughter of

Chronos (Time) and Rhea (Earth). She was the Goddess of the Hearth (Hestia), and represents the domestic hearth of the City, which is grouped round her shrine.

Fire, which was not too readily obtained in primitive times, was looked upon as sacred and its maintenance became the duty of the daughters of each family, whilst engaged in their domestic functions, for the work of maintaining it could not be relegated fittingly to slaves, and the mother of the family had numerous household duties to perform which precluded her from devoting the time and attention necessary to the sacred fire.

When the first cottage was joined by others and a village was formed, a common source of fire was probably established and the task of tending it fell on the daughters of the leading men.

When the village expanded in due course and became a town, or city, the need for a regular organisation arose. As the duty of keeping the sacred fire alight was important and an honour in itself, the early watchers were naturally selected from the Patrician families, but we shall see later how time modified this exclusive selection from the highest caste. The following passage from Lactantius explains the ancient conception of the Virgin Goddess Vesta :

" They (the Stoics) held, he (Cicero) says, that the highest and ethereal nature of heaven, that is, of fire, which by itself produced all things, was without that part of the body which contained the productive organs.

Now this theory might have been suitable to Vesta if she had been called a male. For it is on this account that they esteem Vesta to be a virgin, inasmuch as fire is an inviolable element ; and nothing can be born from it, since it consumes all things, whatever it has seized upon." (Lactantius, *Divin. Inst.*, I, 12.)

Ovid, also, in the *Fasti* (VI, 291), says:

" Nor do you esteem Vesta to be anything else than a living flame and you see no bodies produced from flame. Therefore she is truly a virgin, for she sends forth no seed nor receives it and has the attendants of virginity."

The same idea that the purity and sterility of fire are appropriately tended by virgin ministers is found in Plutarch's account of the establishment of the Order of Vestals, by Numa, religious founder of Rome.

" For they do give Numa the first foundation and consecrating of them, and the institution also of keeping the immortal fire with honour and reverence, which these Vestals have the charge of. Either for that he thought it meet to commit the substance of fire (being pure and clean) unto the custody of clean and uncorrupt maids, or else because he thought the nature of fire (which is barren and bringeth forth nothing), was fittest, and most proper unto virgins." (Plutarch, *Numa*, IX, North's translation.)

Livy's account, pleasantly rendered by Philemon Holland, is worth setting beside it :

" He instituted also a Nunnerie as it were, of religious Vestall virgines. A priesthood that had the beginning from Alba, and suited well with the house, from whom the first founder of the cittie was descended. And to the end that they should attend continually about the church, as resiant chaplaines, he allowed them an ordinarie fee or pension, at the publike charges of the cittie ; and made them by perpetuall vowed virginitie and other ceremonies to be reverenced and accounted holie." (Livy, I, 20.)

Numa is said to have built in 710 B.C. one temple common to all the curiæ or wards of Rome, between the Palatine and Capitoline Hills, which were encompassed by a single wall, while the Forum, in which the temple was placed, lay between them.

As Vesta, who herself typified the earth, was to be regarded as the centre of the universe, so fire, which is sacred to her, was placed in the centre of the City. (Dionysius, II, 66, and Plutarch, *Numa*, XI.)

According to Monsieur André Lefèvre, in his *L'Italie Antique*, colonies used to send to their mother cities for a supply of the sacred flame, and Rome looked with veneration on the fire drawn from its parent city Alba Longa.

Plutarch also refers to the procedure adopted in the case of the Sacred Fire going out accidentally :

" If the fire happen by any accident to be put out, as the sacred lamp is said to have been at Athens, under the tyranny of Aristion ; at Delphi, when the temple was burned by the Medes ; and at Rome in the Mithridatic war, as also in the civil war, when not only the fire was extinguished but the altar overturned ; it is not to be lighted again from another fire, but a new fire is to be gained by drawing a pure and un-polluted flame from the sunbeams.

They kindle it generally with concave vessels of brass, formed by the conic section of a rectangled triangle, whose lines from the circumference meet in one central point. This being placed against the sun, causes its rays to converge in the centre, which, by reflection, acquiring the force and activity of fire, rarefy the air, and immediately kindle such light and dry matter as they think fit to apply." (Plutarch, *Numa*, IX, Langhorne's translation.)

It is interesting to note that the method of rekindling the sacred fire of Peru was similar to that narrated above.

In the following passage, Plutarch goes in detail into the various suggested origins of the Sacred Fire, and the mysteries of the Roman worship, referring specially to the duties of the Vestal Virgins on the occasion when the Gauls were threatening Rome (390 B.C.) :

" They (the Romans) retired to the Capitol, which they fortified with strong ramparts and provided well with arms.

But their first care was of their holy things, most of which they conveyed into the Capitol.

As for the Sacred Fire, the Vestal Virgins took

it up, together with other holy relics, and fled away with it.

Some, however, will have it that they have not the charge of anything but that ever-living fire which Numa appointed to be worshipped as the principle of all things.

It is indeed the most active thing in nature ; and all generation either is motion or, at least, with motion.

Other parts of matter, which when the heat fails, lie sluggish and dead, crave the force of fire as an informing soul, and when that comes, they acquire some active or passive quality.

Hence it was that Numa, a man curious in his researches into Nature, and on account of his wisdom supposed to have conversed with the Muses, consecrated this fire, and ordered it to be perpetually kept up, as an image of that Eternal Power which preserves and actuates the universe. Others say, that according to the usage of the Greeks, the fire is kept ever burning before the Holy Places, as an emblem of purity ; but that here are other things in the most secret part of the Atrium, kept from the sight of all but those Virgins whom they call Vestals ; and the most current opinion is that the Palladium of Troy, which Æneas brought into Italy, is laid up there.

Others say that the Samothracian gods are there concealed ; whom Dardanus, after he had built Troy, brought to that city and caused to be worshipped ; and that after the taking of Troy, Æneas privately carried them off, and kept them till he settled in Italy.

But those who pretend to know most about these matters say that there are placed there two casks of a moderate size, the one open and empty, the other full and sealed up, but neither of them to be seen by any but those holy virgins.

Others, again, think this is all a mistake, which arose from their putting most of their sacred utensils in two casks and hiding them underground in the temple of Quirinus, and that the place is still called Doliola from these casks.

They took, however, with them the choicest and most sacred things they had, and fled with them along the side of the river ; where Lucius Albinus, a plebeian, among others that were making their escape, was carrying his wife and children and some of his most necessary movables in a waggon.

But when he saw the Vestals in a helpless and weary condition, carrying in their arms the sacred symbols of the gods, he immediately took out his family, and goods, and put the Virgins in the waggon, that they might make their escape to some of the Grecian cities.

This piety of Albinus, and the veneration he expressed for the gods at so dangerous a juncture, deserved to be recorded." (Plutarch, *Camillus*, XX, XXI, Langhorne's translation.)

Another version of the story of Albinus and the Vestals, during the flight from the Gauls, is given us by Livy (V, 40, trans. Philemon Holland):

" The Flamen of Quirinus and the religious Vestall virgines, leaving the regard of their owne private affairs, consulted with themselves what sacred images to carry with them, and (seeing that their strength would not serve to rid away and save all) what to leave behind them, and what place was meetest to bestow and lay them up most safely.

They agreed at length, and thought it best, to put them in small barrels or rundelets, and within the ground to burie them in a little chappell, standing next to the Flamines house ; which place for very devotion unto this day, may not for anything be spit upon.

All the rest they parted among themselves. And every one carrying her owne burden, tooke the way, which over the wodden bridge leadeth to Janiculum.

Upon the ascent or rise of that hill, when L. Albinus (a Commoner of Rome) saw them going, as he among other companie (which, unmeet for war, departed out of the cittie), carried his wife and children in a waine ;

he making even then in that hard calamitie a difference yet, between divine and humane things, and thinking it an impious part and void of all religion that the publike priests with the sacred images of the people of Rome should go on foot, whiles he and his, were seene riding at ease in a wagon, caused his wife and children to alight and come forth and set the nuns with their holy images in their roome and brought them to Cære to which place they were minded to go."

Such is the story how the Vestals preserved their sacred objects and fled with the sacred fire to Cære, twenty-seven miles west of Rome. There they performed their sacred functions. (Festus, 44; Valerius Maximus, I, 1, 10.)

A derivation of the word cæremonia is suggested from Cære-memoria (in memory of Cære) ; but might it not be with equal probability from Cære and monere, " to warn ", " put in mind of " ?   (Festus, l.c.)

" The Virgins who serve the goddess were originally four," writes Dionysius, " and elected by the Kings, according to the law established by Numa. But afterwards, from the multiplicity of their functions, their number was increased to six, and has so remained to this day.

They live near the temple of the goddess, into which none are hindered from entering in the day time ; but it is not lawful for any man to remain there in the night. They are under a necessity of continuing unmarried during the space of thirty years ; which they employ in offering sacrifices, and performing other rites, ordained by the law. During their first ten years, their duty was to learn their functions ; in the second ten, to perform them ; and during the remainder of their term, to instruct the younger ones. After the expiration of the term of thirty years, nothing hindered those who desired from marrying, upon giving up their stemmata (garlands) and the other ensigns of their priesthood." (Dionysius, II, 67, trans. E. Spelman 1758.)

" It is reported that at first only two virgins were consecrated by Numa, whose names were Gegania and Verania ; afterwards two others, Canuleia and Tarpeia, were added ; to these Servius added two more ; and that number (six) has continued to this time." (Plutarch, *Numa*, Langhorne's translation.)

Dionysius (III, 67) says it was Tarquin who increased the number to six.

Of the four Vestals appointed by Numa Pompilius, two were chosen from the Titienses, and two from the Ramnes.

The two added later were from the Luceres.

It has been suggested by some authorities that a seventh was added later, but this is doubtful.

Aulus Gellius (I, 12, i), quoting Antistius Labeo, says that at their selection, they were to be perfect of form and in all their senses ; to have both parents living, these being free-born and patricians.

It was also stipulated that they must have been born in Italy, and the daughters of anyone who followed any dishonourable occupation were expressly excluded, and no girl was eligible under 6 or over 10 years of age.

At an early date, the daughters of plebeians were accepted, and afterwards Augustus made a law by which daughters of freedmen became eligible. (Dion Cassius, LV, 22.)

This law was really due to a difficulty in finding candidates ; as many parents began to object to surrendering all parental rights over their daughters.

The Lex Papia ordained that when a vacancy occurred, the Pontifex Maximus should select twenty girls, and from this number, one was elected by ballot, which must be held in public.

A parent could offer his child voluntarily, and then the Senate made the selection if there were more than one candidate. (Tacitus, *Ann.*, II. 86.) In this case a certain candidate whose parents were still living together was preferred to another whose mother had been divorced, and the Emperor dowered her with ten hundred thousand sesterces. (*Ibid.* 19.) Moreover, as stated, a girl was ineligible who stammered (lingua debili) or was deaf or had some other bodily defect. (Aulus Gellius, I, 12, 3.)

When the child was chosen, the High Priest took her by the hand, and thus addressed her, as recorded by Fabius Pictor (in A. Gellius, I, 12, 14[1]).

" That even as the best law has been, so do I take thee, Beloved One, to be a Vestal Priestess, to perform the Sacred Rites, which it is meet for the priestess of Vesta to do for the Roman people and citizens."

By this ceremony she passed from the authority of her father to that of the High Priest.

She was then conducted by the High Priest to the Atrium Vestæ, or Home of the Vestals, and her hair was close cropped, as that of the nuns is now on their taking the veil ; and then was hung on a tree called the Capillata, which grew by the Atrium (Pliny, *N.H.*, XVI, 235 ; Festus, 57.) Next she was robed in the costume of the Vestals, and the shorn hair was bound with a white woollen riband, or fillet, called Vitta. (Dionysius, VIII, 89; Juvenal, IV, 9; Lucan, I, 597.)

" I was at the Ilian flame, when the woollen fillet
 Slipped from my hair, falling before the sacred
  hearth." (Ovid, *F.*, III, 30.)

The word " Amata ", used in this Ceremony of Initiation, which seems inappropriate when applied to a little child, requires explanation.

There can be little doubt that it might be freely translated, " the chosen of the Lord," in order to reveal its full significance, historical and religious.

The wife of King Latinus, the traditional ancestor, of the Alban dynasty, was called Amata, as was also the first Vestal Virgin, according to Aulus Gellius

---

[1] " Sacerdotem Vestalem, quæ sacra faciat, quæ jus siet sacerdotem Vestalem facere pro populo Romano Quiritibus, uti quæ optima lege fuit, ita te, Amata, capio."

(I, 12), and it is quite evident that in the earlier traditions of the Cult, the Vestal Virgins were regarded as the possible brides of the Deity as well as the priestesses of his rites.

This idea of a god espousing a virgin of earth, is common to the beginnings of religion in every part of the world.[1] There is therefore a certain grim irony in the story of Heliogabalus at a later date, taking a Vestal Virgin temporarily to wife after he had proclaimed himself to be the only true god of the Romans.

When the Vestal had passed through all the grades of priestess and had served her thirty years, she became by rotation Virgo Vestalis Maxima, or High Vestal Virgin—Lady Superior. " Quæ natu maxima virgo." (Ovid, *Fasti*, IV, 639.)

Tacitus (*Ann.*, 86) speaks of Occia in A.D. 19 having presided over the sacred ceremonies of the Vestals for fifty-seven years.

Junia Torquata was 64 years of age, when she became High Vestal. (Gruter, Vol. I, XXV, 10.) Clœlia Torquata ruled the Order over thirty years, from A.D. 225 to 257. Flavia Publicia presided from A.D. 257 till after 283.

---

[1] Compare Genesis vi. 2 : " The sons of God saw the daughters of men that they were fair, and they took them wives of all which they chose."

THE RELIGIOUS DUTIES OF THE VESTALS

LIVY, as recorded previously, describes the Order of the Vestals as, " a Nonnerie as it were of religious Vestall virgines."

He goes on to say that Numa constituted them " to the end that they should attend continually about the church as resiant chapelaines " and, " allowed them an ordinarie fee or pension at the public charge of the cittie ; and made them by perpetuall vowed virginitie and other ceremonies to be reverenced and accounted holie." (Livy, I, 20, translated by Philemon Holland.)

Plutarch has also placed it on record how great importance was believed to have attached to the exact performance of religious rites :

" Numa was of opinion that his citizens should neither see nor hear any religious service in a slight or careless way, but disengaged from other affairs, bring with them that attention which an object of such importance required." (Plutarch, *Numa*, Langhorne's translation.)

He appointed the Pontifex Maximus to see that all rites were properly observed.

" He had also the inspection of the holy virgins called Vestals."

It may be taken that the service of the Vestals was carried out with the same meticulous care.

" For to Numa is ascribed the sacred establishment of the Vestal Virgins and the whole service with regard to the perpetual fire, which they watch continually."

We know also that they had the duty of guarding this sacred fire and conveying it to the various temples for the sacrifices and lights, and of drawing and carrying all the water needed for the service of the temples with which they were concerned. They had also to supply the salt-wafer (mola salsa), and the salt sprinkled over the victims, but it must be remembered that they took no part in living sacrifices.

They had to attend certain state religious ceremonies during the year beside their own peculiar rites. A list with descriptions of these ceremonies is given later on.

Plutarch (*ib.*) says :

" Some are of opinion that the Sacred Virgins have the care of nothing but the perpetual fire. But others say that they have some private rites besides, kept from the sight of all but their own Order."

They had also the charge of the Palladium and of certain other holy relics. They and the Salii, or priests of Mars, had between them the care of all the sacred objects of Rome. They had also the duty of offering public prayers, as is shown by the following passage from Cicero's oration, " Pro Fonteio " (chap. XVII), when he was defending M. Fonteius against a charge of extortion in his province of Gaul.

After dealing with the specific charges, Cicero asks the jury whether they will allow a Gaulish chief before their eyes to drag the defendant from the embraces of his mother, and that too, when his sister, a Vestal Virgin, is clinging to his other side, a Vestal " who has for so many years been engaged in prayers to the immortal gods for you and for your children so that she may now gain your sympathies for herself and her brother. What protection, what consolation will be left to this poor woman, when her brother is lost to her ?

For other women can themselves give birth to men to defend them and can have them in their homes as their partners and sharers of their fortunes. What happiness or pleasure can this virgin have except from her brother ?

Gentlemen, do not suffer the altars of the immortal gods and of Mother Vesta to be reminded by your verdict of the daily lamentations of the virgin. Look to it that that eternal fire, which has been preserved by the nightly toil and watching of Fonteia, be not said to have been quenched by the tears of your Priestess. The Vestal Virgin stretches to you those same suppliant hands which she has been wont to stretch on your behalf to the immortal gods."

An experienced advocate like Cicero would never have ventured on a piece of special pleading like this, if it had not been a matter of common knowledge in Rome that public prayers were really offered by the Vestals and of common belief that those prayers were efficacious.

The commentator, Servius, in a note on Vergil (*Æneid*, Book X, 228), refers to the following passage:

" Art thou on the watch, heaven-born Æneas ? Keep watch."

These words, he says, are those of the ritual ; for on an appointed day the virgins of Vesta used to go to the King of the religious rites (Rex Sacrorum) and say, " Art thou on the watch, O King ? Keep watch."

The worship of Fascinus also was entrusted to the Vestal Virgins. In this connection, Pliny writes :

" The god protecting infants and generals was Fascinus, a divinity whose worship is entrusted to the Vestal Virgins, and forms part of the Roman rites. It is the image of this divinity that is attached beneath the triumphal chariot of the victorious general, protecting it like some attendant physician, against the effects of envy." (Pliny, *N.H.*, XXVIII, 39.)

In processions the image of Janus came first ; the Vestals probably were in the rear.

Cicero (*De natura deorum*, II, 27) writes :

" Vis eius (Vestæ) ad aras et focos pertinet. Atque in ea dea quæ est rerum custos intimarum, omnis et precatio et sacrificatio extrema est."

" Her power relates to altars and hearths. Consequently in the case of that goddess, who is the guardian of secret things, all prayer and sacrifice alike come last."

In addition to the various duties recorded above, the Vestal Virgins were expected to attend certain annual Roman Festivals, and other functions, including :—

February 13th. Parentatio. Worship of the dead at Tomb of the Vestal Tarpeia.

February 15th. The Lupercalia. Using up of the last of the salt-wafers.

February 17th. The Fornacalia. (Pliny, *N.H.*, XVIII, 8. Ovid, *F.*, II, 525–7.) In honour of Fornax, goddess of ovens, that the baking of the corn might be successful.

March 1st. The sacred fire re-kindled.[1]

March 6th. Sacrifice to Vesta. Augustus elected Pontifex Maximus.

March 16th and 17th. Visit to Sacra Argeorum (the twenty-four places consecrated by Numa for religious services).

April 15th. The Fordicidia. Pregnant cows are sacrificed, and the High Vestal burns the calves, that the people may be purified on the festival of Pales.

April 21st. The Parilia. Anniversary of the foundation of Rome.

April 28th. Foundation by Augustus of a Temple to Vesta on the Palatine (Anniversary.)

May 1st. Rites of the Bona Dea. (Also on Dec. 3rd and 4th.)

May 7th–15th. The three elder Vestal Virgins plucked the first ears of corn for their sacramental cake (mola salsa).

---

[1] On this occasion, the Pontifex Maximus extinguished the fire and re-kindled it with the aid of the Vestal Virgins probably in the chapel (locus intimus). On this day, the Vestals also renewed the laurels which decorated their shrine (ædes Vestæ).

May 15th.	Vestals throw the Argei, (straw men,) into the Tiber. (Ovid, *F.*, V, 621.)
June 9th.	Festival of Vesta. (Opening of the Penus Vestæ to the matrons.)
June 15th.	The sweepings of the Temple thrown down the Porta Stercoraria.
August 21st.	Festival of Consus, god of counsel and harvest.
August 25th.	Festival of Ops Consiva, the goddess of seed time.
Sept. 13th.	Festival of Jupiter.
October 15th.	Sacrifice of the October horse (see p. 120).
Dec. 3rd. & 4th (about).	Rites of the Bona Dea.

THE SACRED FIRE

IT has been stated (p. 28) that the Sacred Fire was re-kindled annually by the Pontifex Maximus, assisted of the Vestal Virgins.

The whole question of kindling sacred fire is of the greatest interest in itself, inasmuch as one finds, quite apart from the well-known actual Fire Worshipping religions, analogous cults in all parts of the world, with identical methods of obtaining the fire and a ritual with very small differences in detail, but a generally similar significance.

To appreciate this fact in its proper perspective, it must be remembered that the subject of procreation was ever uppermost in the outlook of all early races, a primitive necessity in the struggle for existence, entirely innocent of pruriency, a tribute, religious in fact, to the importance of propagating the species, not so much a natural impulse as a national necessity.

Amongst the Indians of North America, the West African natives, the Bedouins of the desert, the Hereros of South Africa, and even the aborigines of Central Australia, one finds not merely the same two-stick methods as those of ancient Rome, but in every case a sexual construction and significance is given to the actual sticks used for obtaining the primitive fire.

In their various languages they are called the male and the female, and their shapes and functions are imitative of the human anatomy.

To the primitive mind, the slave of imagination and symbolism, the fire produced was as much the child of the male and female sticks as the infant in the wattle hut was the offspring of its parents.

New life, in all its forms, was the promise of the future, the crystallisation of the hopes of the present for a noble posterity, hence in its inception it became an object of veneration, a fact worthy to be worshipped.

THE LUPERCALIA

THE Festival of the Lupercalia (15th February) is of particular interest, especially as the use of a salt wafer (mola salsa) is one of its principal features.

The Luperci were priests of Pan, their origin being ascribed to Numa. They had to sacrifice dogs and goats to their special deity.

This festival was held in February, which month has its name from Februo=I purify.

The people assembled at the " Lupercal," a cave at the foot of the S.W. corner of the Palatine ; the word seems and was popularly held to be connected with Lupus, a wolf, in commemoration of the wolf that suckled Romulus and Remus.

Sacrifice was made of goats and dogs, which were quite unusual victims, to mark, perhaps, the solemnity of the occasion. A feature of the sacrifice was the mola salsa (salt wafer), which had been prepared by the Vestals from the earliest ears of the last year's harvest.

Two youths of high rank, one from each of the two colleges of Luperci, were brought forward and their foreheads were smeared with blood, which was partially wiped off with wool and milk. The ceremony was conducted with much laughter, and this was regarded as essential.

These two noble youths were each at the head of a company of young men. After an ample banquet, they ran round the Palatine carrying strips of skin (februa) taken from the victims. With these they belaboured any women they met.

The following passage from Shakespeare (*Julius Cæsar*, Act I, Sc. 2) explains the reason for this custom:

Cæsar. " Calphurnia ! "
Calp. " Here, my Lord."

Cæs.   " Stand you directly in Antonius' way,
         When he doth run his course.—Antonius!"
Ant.   " Cæsar, my Lord."
Cæs.   " Forget not in your speed, Antonius,
         " To touch Calphurnia ; for our elders say,
         " The barren, touched in this holy chase,
         " Shake off their sterile curse."

Cicero (*Phil.*, II, 84) refers to the behaviour of Antony at this feast :

" But lest by chance, out of a long list of actions of Antony my speech should miss one most priceless incident, let us proceed to the Lupercalia.

He makes no concealment, My Lords.

It seems that he is embarrassed ; he is sweating, he is pale. Let him do anything he likes so long as he does not vomit as he did in the Porch of Minucius.

What excuse can there be for such a disgusting act ? I want to hear, in order to see where the enormous wage he paid his oratorical tutor comes in. Your colleague was sitting on the rostrum, draped in a purple gown on a golden seat, crowned with a wreath." (Then comes the famous offer of the crown to Cæsar.)

(*Ib.*, III, 12.) " And certainly you ought not to have counted Antony as consul after the Lupercalia ; for on that day, in full view of the Roman public, naked, perfumed, drunk, he made his speech and he did so to place the crown on the head of his colleague.

On that day, he resigned not only the consulship but even his claim to freedom." (Latin text, see Appendix I.)

Plutarch (*Cæsar*, 61) describes the licentious proceedings at the Lupercalia as follows :

" Of the noble youths and magistrates, many run up through the city half naked, in shaggy hides and striking those who meet them by way of sport and joke."

Plutarch appears to have overlooked the religious belief contained in this custom that the touch of the whips (februa) would make the barren women fertile.

THE MOLA SALSA WAFER

AS already stated, the use of the salt wafer (mola salsa) was an integral part of the ceremonies connected with the Festival of the Lupercalia. The mola salsa was a salted cake or wafer made from parched spelt, a sort of rough wheat still grown in the more mountainous districts of Europe.

It was first introduced into Rome by the Sabine king Numa as a propitiation to the gods, looked upon as a bloodless sacrifice, and performed at religious weddings, when a pig was not offered.

" Numa first established the custom of offering corn to the gods, and of propitiating them with the salted cake." (Pliny, *N.H.*, XVIII, 7.)

Remembering the ancient origin of the Sabines, it is a matter of considerable interest to speculate as to the extent to which eastern religions have influenced the early Roman cult.

We know that when Cyrus overcame Nabonidus (555–538 B.C.), the fire-worshipping religion of Zoroaster was fully established, and overcame the religions of the Assyrians.

Zoroastrianism had priests, temples and an altar on which the sacred fire burnt always.

The probable date of Zoroaster is as far back as 1000 B.C., and it is not unlikely that nomadic tribes came in touch with its teachings and carried some of them to Rome.

At a later date, we know that Mithraism, which was an offshoot of Zoroastrianism, became very fashionable in Rome. It was introduced after the Eastern campaigns of Pompey the Great.

Ovid, *F.*, II, 19, says these atoning sacrifices (piamina) were called Februa, and that the parched spelt, with the grain of salt, was also called Februa ; also that it gave its name to the second month.

The remains of the salt mill are yet to be seen in the house of the Vestals, who likewise made the salt cake from the first ears of each harvest (Servius, *ad Ecl.*, VIII, 82) on February 15th.

These cakes were sprinkled over the head of the animal sacrificed, by crumbling. (Servius, *ad Æn.*, IV, 57.)

The Latin word "immolare", originally from "mola", meant to sprinkle the victim for sacrifice, hence to sacrifice, and from it we get the English word to "immolate."

But it is interesting to note that apparently this cake offering can be traced to the East. Read Leviticus ii. 4–16, and see also the sacrificial tablet of Baal in the Marseilles Museum.

"The Jews made cakes to the Queen of Heaven in worship of her." (Jeremiah vii. 18 ; xliv. 19.)

The victim slain, was called "hostia," from "hostio," "I strike."

Chambers's English Dictionary also gives "hostia" (a victim) as the derivation of "host," the consecrated bread of the Eucharist in the Roman Catholic Church.

Yet we are told to "abstain from meats offered to idols !" This seems to be a remnant of the old totemistic religion, the totem being eaten, whereby the worshippers became partakers of the substance of their god on very solemn occasions. It is curious how these old-time customs still exist ; the round wafer used in the Mass being the mola salsa of the Vestals.

Truly, there is nothing new under the sun !

The idea of transubstantiation, or "the real presence," apparently was started by a monk, Paschasius Radbertus, of Corbey, A.D. 831. It was made a belief at the Council of Placentia in 1095, and a hundred years later, Innocent III (1198–1216) pronounced it a doctrine of the Church.

At the Council of Trent, 11th October, 1551, it was declared a dogma of the Church.

The legend of the doubting Bohemian priest pressing the consecrated wafer at Bolsena, and blood oozing out, is dated 1263. As a corollary to this, Urban IV thereupon instituted the festival of the Corpus Domini.

This dogma has never been fully accepted in Britain, though it was admitted before 1547. It is difficult to find out the exact time when the pagan wafer was substituted for bread in the Mass ; probably from the council of Placentia in 1095.

In all the early pictorial representations of the Lord's Supper, of the supper at Emmaus, of the supper of the seven at the lake of Tiberias, and of the Agapé feasts, small loaves are represented, like the English bun, or the Italian pagnottelle. The fresco in the lower church of St. Clemente, about 1050, represents the chalice and a small round pagnottella.

Raphael's fresco of the so-called Disputa, 1511, shows the wafer or hostia ; the oldest representation of which, I believe, is in the frescoes by Ugolino di Prete Itario, frescoed on the walls of the chapel of the San Corporale in the Cathedral at Orvieto, 1337. There is no wafer shown in the frescoes of the Catacombs, and it is in fact a mediæval invention, as far as the Christian Church is concerned, borrowed from the ancient observance of the Vestal Virgins.

THE DROWNING OF THE DUMMIES

(ARGEI)

A S noted above, this curious ceremony took place
annually on the 15th May.

On this occasion the Chief Priest (Pontifex
Maximus), accompanied by the Prætor and another
Magistrate, the Flaminica Dialis (in mourning),
and the Vestals, went in procession to the Pons
Sublicius.

Straw or rush dummies in human form were carried
and thrown by the Vestals into the Tiber. These dummies had been stored and probably prepared in the
ARGEA SACELLA of which there were twenty-four, six for
each of the four regions of the City.

These chapels, with their contents had been in-
spected on March 16th and 17th. (p. 28.)

The fullest account of this ceremony is that given
by Ovid (*Fasti*, V, 621.) Mention is also made of these
ceremonies by Dionysius (I, 38) ; Lactantius (I, 21
citing Varro as his authority) ; Festus (p. 334, *sub voce*
SEXAGENARIOS) ; and Plutarch (*Q.R.*, 32, 86).

Lactantius in the passage cited is speaking of human
sacrifices, in this case not on the altar but thrown from
the Sublician Bridge.

This practice, he says, was abolished by Hercules,
who substituted men of straw. He quotes Varro as an
authority. The passage of Lactantius, including the
quotation from Varro is annexed.

Ovid, as might be expected from him, devotes himself to making an effective story of the matter. Here
is a translation of his account.

He has been relating the story of Jupiter and Europa,
and then launches forth into the legend of the Argei :

" Then too, the maiden is wont from the oaken

bridge, to hurl images in rushwork of men of old time. He who has believed that bodies after six times ten years (of life) were hurled to death, does, by his charge, condemn his ancestors of crime.

The tale is an ancient one.

Once, when the land was called Saturnia, these were the words of the prophetic deity :

'O nations, send two bodies as an offering to the old man with the scythe to be swept down to the Tuscan waves. Till the hero of Tiryns came to these fields, each year the gloomy rites were fulfilled in the Leucadian fashion. 'Tis said that he (Hercules) cast into the water Quirites of straw ; and that from Hercules' example dummy bodies were thrown in.

Some think that the young men hurled frail old men from the bridges, so that the youths might have the sole right to vote. Tell us, O Tiber, the truth ; thy bank is older than the City ; thou mayest well know the origin of the rite.'

(Father) Tiber reared his reed-clad head from mid-channel and with words like these parted his hoarse lips : 'This country have I seen as untenanted grass-land with no city walls ; either bank was feeding straggling cattle and I, Tiber, whom now the peoples know and revere, was food for contempt even to the herds. The name of Arcadian Evander is often on your lips ; he was a stranger who with his oars clove my waters. Came too, Alcides (Hercules), thronged by a Grecian crowd ; then, if I remember, my name was Albula. The Pallantian (Arcadian) hero welcomed the youth with hospitable greeting and at long last the o'er-due punishment came for Cacus. The victor departs and with him leads away the Erythean plunder. But his comrades refuse to go further. Many of their number had left Argos to come here. They place their hopes and homes on these mountains ; yet often are they touched by yearning for their dear home-land and one of them in death, orders this brief behest.

" Cast me into Tiber, that borne by Tiber's waters I

may travel, lifeless clay to Inachia's strand." The charge of the funeral trust pleases not the heir. The dead stranger is buried in the Ausonian (Italian) land. For the dead lord, a figure of rush, is cast into Tiber to seek the Grecian home through the endless seas.'" (Ovid, *Fast.*, V, 621–660.)

The following is a translation of the extract from Lactantius (I, 21) :

" It seems, however, that this style of sacrificing human victims is an ancient one, if as a matter of fact Saturn was ever worshipped in Latium by this same kind of sacrifice, I mean not by a man being sacrificed at the altar, but by his being thrown into the Tiber from the Sublician bridge."

And that this was the practice, is supported by an oracle quoted by Varro, of which the last line is as follows :

" And send down souls to Hades and a mortal man to Pluto."

An interesting incident was the attendance at the ceremony of the Priestess of Jupiter (Flaminica Dialis) clad in mourning robes instead of her usual festive garments. Did this funereal appearance signify regret for the passing of the aged, venerated possibly, but useless because worn out, whilst the casting of the straw figures by the Vestal Virgins into the river typified a regeneration and cleansing by actual immersion in the Tiber.

I think these rites were undoubtedly symbolic of the above ideas. For the welfare of the State was held by the Roman people to depend to a remarkable extent upon the meticulous observance by the Vestals of certain rites, with official attendance and activities at State ceremonies and functions, such as this one of the Argeii.

Lactantius then continues :

" About the children who used to be sacrificed to Saturn on account of his hatred for Jupiter, I cannot find anything to say. For men to have been so barbarous and brutal as to give this parricide of theirs the name of sacrifice, is an offence horrible and repulsive to the human race."

Dionysius of Halicarnassus also writes :

" On which day the Pontiffs, as they are called, the most distinguished of the priests, after first offering the sacrifices prescribed by law, and with them, the Virgins who guard the eternal fire, and the consuls, and those of the other citizens for whom it is lawful to be present, cast from the Sacred Bridge into the stream of the Tiber images fashioned in the likeness of the forms of men, to the number of thirty, calling them Argei." (I, 38, translated by Ed. Spelman.)

This odd ceremony has naturally attracted Plutarch in his *Romane Questions*.

" What is the reason," he asks, " that in the moneth of May, they use at Rome to cast over their woodden bridge into the river, certaine images of men, which they call Argeos ? Is it in memoriall of the Barbarians who sometimes inhabited these parts, and did so by the Greeks, murdering them in that maner as many of them as they could take ? But Hercules, who was highly esteemed among them for his vertue, abolished this cruell fashion of killing of strangers, and taught them this custom to counterfeit their ancient superstitions, and to fling these images in stead of them.

Now in the old time, our ancestors used to name all Greeks of what countrey soever they are, Argeos : unlesse haply a man would say, that the Arcadians reputing the Argives to be their enemies, for that they were their neighbour borderers, such as fled with Evander out of Arcadia, and came to inhabit these quarters, reteined still, the old hatred and rancker, which time out of minde had taken root, and beene settled in their hearts against the said Argives."

(From the original translation and spelling of Philemon Holland.)

Ovid, as usual, takes the obvious way out of his difficulties ; he explains the word " Argeus " as " Argive."

Mr. Warde Fowler prefers to seek affinities in the Greek word, " argos " (white, gleaming), and the good Latin words " argentum," " argilla," offer a reasonable correspondence. He interprets " Argei " as the " white ones " or the " old ones."

In this connexion, Ovid's reference to the notion that the ceremony relates to the idea of throwing old men over the bridge, echoes a common Roman catch-word, " sexagenarios de ponte," which was familiar as an election cry at Rome.

Men of over sixty were not supposed to enter the polling booths (septa), and the cry meant that they were to be thrust back from the pontes or gangways which led to them. (Varro, *Ap Non.*, 523.)

(See also Cicero, *Pro Roscio Amerino*, XXXV.)

An ancient custom was that on March 14th, a man got up in skins to represent an old man, was beaten with long white rods and expelled from the neighbourhood. The name given him was MAMURIUS VETURIUS.[1]

A more probable explanation is that of Mr. Warde Fowler, that the whole idea of the drowning of the dummy old men typifies Nature's annual supersession of dead matter by new life.

He further suggests that it was a use of " sympathetic magic," exercised by the Vestal Virgins, probably to secure rain.

There is no doubt the people of Rome credited the Vestals with magic powers.

Pliny (*N.H.*, XXVIII, 13) tells us that in his time, it was believed that a slave who had run away could be stopped by a spell cast over him by one of the Vestal Virgins, provided he was still in the city. It was thought that their state of virginity augmented the potency of the spell.

---

[1] There is a similar Slav custom of " Carrying out Death."

THE FORDICIDIA AND THE PARILIA

AT the festival of the Fordicidia on the 15th of April each year, a sacrifice of pregnant cows was made to Mother Earth.

The unborn calves were taken and burnt by the Chief Vestal, the ashes being kept for use at the Shepherds' Festival of the Parilia (21st of April). At the Parilia the Vestal Virgins mixed these ashes with the blood of a horse which had been kept for a sacrifice in the previous October, and this strange mixture was distributed to the Shepherds.

It was used by them to fumigate or disinfect their flocks. This was believed to ensure the fertility of the dams, and a plentiful supply of milk.

In this connection one is struck by the apparent anomaly of the Vestal Virgins being concerned in ceremonies designed to promote the propagation of species, animal or vegetable.

The only explanation is to give confirmation to the original idea that the Virgins, who may not mate with men, were regarded as the brides of the Sacred Fire, the manifestation of the God.

Vesta herself, as previously stated, was worshipped, not as a Virgin, but as Mother Vesta, the Goddess of Fruitfulness, who bestowed offspring on woman and cattle.

The story of the birth of Servius Tullius illustrates this conception.

Ocrisia, it is related, the slave girl of Queen Tanaquil, wife of Tarquinius Priscus, was tending the fire one day when suddenly a flame leaped out on the hearth.

Queen Tanaquil, observing the significant form of the flame, which to her eyes resembled the male organ of generation, took it to be a sign from Heaven, and commanded the maiden to array herself in her bridal robes, as she was destined to be the mate of the God.

The maiden obeyed, the flame again appeared to her in the same shape, and a son was born to her, who was Servius Tullius. (Plutarch, *de Fort. Rom.*, 10 ; Pliny, *N.H.*, XXXVI, 204 ; Ovid, *Fasti*, VI, 627 *et seq.*)

Preller (*Römische Mythologie*, II, 344) implies that the mother of Servius Tullius was probably a Vestal Virgin charged with the custody and worship of the Sacred Fire in the King's house.

A similar legend is related of the birth of Romulus, so that the general idea is apparent that the early Roman kings were born of a pure virgin by the Spirit of Fire.

Sir James Frazer (*Golden Bough*, Pt. i, Vol. II, p. 229) traces a connection, more than a mere coincidence, between this Roman Shepherd Festival of the Parilia, and the Festival on the 23rd of April (two days later than the Parilia) dedicated to the much-worshipped St. George in Eastern Europe, the patron saint of cattle, horses and wolves.

St. George is largely mythical, but there is a strong degree of probability in the tradition that he was a Roman officer of high rank who fell a martyr to his faith just before the triumph of Christianity. If one accepts this tradition, the link with old Roman customs becomes more intelligible.

The fact that St. George's reputed tomb was near the spot where Perseus rescued Andromeda would explain the introduction of the Dragon into the legend.

FESTIVAL OF VESTA

THE Festival of Vesta was held on the 9th of June. The ceremonies commenced on the 5th and closed on the 15th, and were kept as religious days.

Propertius, speaking of the early days of Rome, says (V, 1, 21) : "Vesta was then poor, and content with a procession of wreathed asses," upon her festival.

There was a tradition that the ass of Silenus, braying on a certain occasion and thus awakening her, saved Vesta from an awkward position, and the too ardent attentions of Priapus. So on her festival, the grateful goddess adorned the ass with a garland made of loaves, when the mill-stones, in idleness, cease their grating noise—that is, the donkeys had a rest.

Ovid (*Fasti*, VI, 311–348) tells this story ; and at the Vestalia, he says :

" Behold ! the garlands of bread hang down from the asses, and the floral wreaths cover the rough mill-stones."

It may be this custom explains the promise in the graffito formerly in the Domus Gelotiana of the Palatine, where an ass was represented as working a mill, the master standing by, saying, " Work, little ass, as I have worked myself, and it shall profit thee."

Unfortunately, the damp got behind the stucco, and it fell off the wall in 1886. It was of the time of Gordianus III, whose portrait adjoined it.

Perhaps this alludes to the origin of the donkey worship attributed by the Romans to the Jews and early Christians.

Ovid speaks of attending the festival, and gives us some topographical information :

44

" By chance, I was returning, at the festival of Vesta,
   by the street where the Forum Romanum is
   now joined to the Via Nova.
Hither I saw a matron descending with bare feet :
I was astonished and said nothing, and restrained my
   step.
An old woman of the adjoining locality, noticing me
   and
Shaking her head, addressed me with tremulous
   voice and ordered me to sit down."

(Ovid, F., VI, 395.)

She explains to Ovid why the matron had her feet
bare, but it had nothing to do with Vesta. The street
he speaks of as now joining the Forum to the Via Nova
was possibly the Vicus Bublarius, which runs out of
the Forum under the east side of the Temple of
Castor.

CIVIL DUTIES OF THE VESTAL VIRGINS

IN addition to their religious duties, the Vestals were often entrusted with wills, treaties and other important documents, as well as with treasure. The wills of the Emperors were generally lodged with them. As far as I can judge, this custody was voluntary on the part of the Vestals and regarded as a compliment to them.

The following passages refer to the practice :

" The will which Julius Cæsar had made on the preceding 13th September on his estate at Lavicum and had entrusted to the Chief Vestal." (Suetonius, *Cæsar*, 83.)

Cæsar was murdered on the 15th March, so the Vestals had it for six months.

The following allusions in Tacitus and Suetonius also refer to the same duty :

" Augusti, cuius testamentum inlatum per virgines Vestæ Tiberium et Liviam heredes habuit." (Tacitus, *Ann.*, I, 8.)

. . . " of Augustus, whose will, which was brought in by the Vestal Virgins, constituted Tiberius and Livia as his heirs."

Dr. Furneaux, in a note, states that " wills, treaties and other documents, and money " were deposited with the Vestals.

" His (Augustus') last will and testament made by him when L. Plancus and C. Silius were consuls, the third day before the Nones of April, a yeere and foure months before he died, and the same in two bookes written partly with his own hand and in part with the hands of Polibus and Hilarius his freedmen, the Vestal virgins, who had the keeping thereof upon trust, brought forth, together with three other rolls or volumes sealed alike." (Suetonius, *Augustus*, 101, translated by Philemon Holland.)

Holland has a pretty footnote :

" In the custody of the Vestall virgins or votaries as Julius Cæsar had done before him. Of such integritie and so good a conscience were they thought to be, as things of greatest weight were committed to them in trust."

Again on a treaty between Sex. Pompeius and Augustus :

" They agreed to the conditions and drew up this document and signed it and sent it to Rome to the holy virgins to keep." (Appian, *Civil War*, V, 73 ; Dio Cassius, XLVIII, 37.)

The sanctity of the Vestals, however, did not prevent Augustus forcibly removing from them the will of Antony and reading it with adverse comments to the Senate, who were shocked at this breach of the Vestals' inviolability. (Plutarch, *Ant.* 58, *cp*. Dio Cassius, L, 3.)

The following passage from Plutarch (M. Cato XX, 5) shows the respect in which they were held: " He (Cato) sayed also that he tooke as great heade for any fowle or uncomely words before his sonne as he would have donne if he had bene before the Vestall Nunnes."   (North's trans.)

PRIVILEGES OF THE VESTALS

OF all the institutions of Rome, the Foundation of the Vestals appeared to the average Roman to represent more than anything else the immemorial majesty of the City.

Horace, wishing for some instance of an institution which had existed from the beginning of Time and was likely to continue to the end of it, says, " Dum Capitolium scandet cum tacita virgine Pontifex."

" So long as the Priest mounts the Capitol with the silent virgin," and in every aspect of life, we have evidence of the deep reverence and respect in which the Vestals were held.

Vergil, in the well-known prophecy from the first book of the *Æneid*, also writes :

" Aspera tum positis mitescent sæcula bellis,
    Cana Fides et Vesta, Remo cum fratre Quirinus
        Iura dabunt."

" Then, when wars shall be no more, the cruelty of the Ages shall grow gentle. Time-honoured Faith with Vesta, Quirinus and Remus his brother, shall be the lawgivers."

Plutarch, for example, writes :

" The King (Numa) honoured them with great privileges, such as the power to make a will during their father's life, and to transact other affairs without a guardian, like the mother of three boys now."

When they went out, they had the right to have a lictor, carrying the fasces, to march before them ; and if, by accident, they met a person being led to execution, his life was spared, always subject to an affirmation that there had been no collusion, but death was the penalty for him who passed under the litter. (Plutarch, *Numa*, 10 ; Dio Cassius, XLVII, 19.)

Even Consuls and Prætors made way for them and lowered their fasces (Seneca, *Controvers.*, VI, 3), much as a modern ship dips its flag in salute, or soldiers honour authority by presenting arms.

Suetonius tells us that the Vestal Virgins could in some cases override the power of the Tribunes. He writes :

" Furthermore, a virgine vestale was there of that name (Claudia), who when a brother of hers received a ' Triumph ', without a warrant from the people, mounted up with him into the chariot, and accompanied him even into the Capitoll, to this end that none of the Tribunes might lawfully oppose themselves and forbid the Triumph." (Suetonius, *Tiberius*, 2, Holland's translation.)

Holland has a footnote :

" Of so reverend regard were these Nunnes, that no magistrate might either attach or crosse them."

And again :

" Donec per virgines vestales perque Mam: Æmilium et Aurelium Cottam propinquos et adfines suos veniam impetravit." (Suetonius, *Cæsar*, I.)

" Until through the intermediary of the Vestal Virgins, and of his relatives and neighbours, M. Æmilius and Aurelius Cotta, he obtained a pardon."

The reference is to Cæsar, who had married a daughter of Marius, the democratic leader, and when called upon by Sulla to divorce her, had refused. He was heavily fined, but escaping, left Rome, and shifted his quarters daily, bribing his pursuers, until through the mediation of the Vestal Virgins, Æmilius, and Aurelius Cotta, he was pardoned.

The point of this reference is that it shows that the social and political influence of the Vestals could be classed with that of well-known men like those mentioned.

Special traffic privileges were also accorded to the Vestal Virgins.

Georg Wissowa on p. 508 of his *Religion und Kultus der Römer*, makes the following statement :

D

" The Lex Julia Municipalis (C.I.L., I. 206) allows the use of carriages in the city—' quibus diebus virgines Vestales regem sacrorum flamines plostreis in urbe sacrorum publicorum populi Romani causa vehi oportebit ' "—i.e., " on the days on which it will be proper for the Vestal Virgins, the Rex Sacrorum and the Flamens to ride in carriages in the city for the purpose of the public rites of the Roman people."

This law (enacted in 45 B.C.) prohibited vehicular traffic in the streets of Rome for the first ten hours of the day from sunrise, as well as at other crowded times, an exception being made in favour of persons engaged in the erection or demolition of public buildings and temples, Vestals, Flamens, the Rex Sacrorum and generals who were receiving a public triumph.

Wissowa cites also Tacitus (*Annals*, XII, 42):

" Suum quoque fastigium Agrippina extollere altius; Capitolium carpento ingredi, qui honos, sacerdotibus et sacris antiquitus concessus venerationem augebat feminæ."

" Agrippina also raised her own dignity higher ; she entered the Capitol in a two-wheeled chariot, an honour which had from very early days been allowed to priests and to the sacred emblems and which increased the celebrity of the woman."

He quotes also Livy (I, 21), to the effect that Numa established a chapel at which he used to meet Egeria, and ordered the Flamens to drive to it in two-wheeled chariots and carry out their rites. It is also mentioned that he founded the Argean processions.

Wissowa further mentions that Vestals had the right to intramural burial :

" They alone of all the priests and priestesses have a right to burial inside the city." (Servius on *Æn.* XI, 206.)

Aulus Gellius (X, 15) states that Vestals had the right of giving evidence[1] in a Court of Justice, without taking the oath. This distinction was first granted to

[1] The Alban Vestals gave evidence at Milo's trial in 52 B.C. (Asconius).

a certain Caia Taracia or Fufetia, and afterwards extended to all Vestal Virgins. (Aul. Gell., VII, 7, 2.) It was she who presented to the public a field bordering on the Tiber and had a statue erected to her. (Pliny, *N.H.*, XXXIV, 25.) Further, they had the right to bequeath their property by will independently of wardship and, generally speaking, of being free from any wardship whatever. (Gaius. I, 145 ; Plutarch, *Numa*, 10, and Gellius, VII, 7, 2.)

Thus writes the last named :—

" Ius quoque testimonii dicendi tribuitur testabilisque una omnium feminarum ut sit datur "—" The right also of giving evidence is granted to her, and it is allowed that she, alone of all women, shall be capable of making a will."[1]

Gellius also says (I, 12, 9), " ius testamenti faciendi adipiscitur "—" she obtains the right of making a will."

The privilege of special seats at the Gladiatorial Games was also accorded to the Vestals, contrary to the usual rule that Roman women occupied the uppermost (i.e. the worst) seats at the Games.

The Vestal Virgins, however, and at a later date, ladies of the Imperial family, were specially allotted front seats.

In this connection, Suetonius says :

" As for women, he (Augustus) would not allow them to behold so much as the sword fencers (gladiatores)—who customarily in the time past were to be seene of all indifferently—but from some higher loft above the rest, sitting there by themselves. To the Vestall Nunnes, he graunted a place apart from the rest within the theatre, and the same just over against the Prætour's tribunall. Howbeit from the sollemnitie of Champion-shew, he banished all the female sex. so farre forth as that during the Pontificall Games, he put off a couple of them who were called for to enter in to combat, untill the morrow morning. And made

---

[1] According to Pauly, only the Vestals could give evidence without being sworn. According to Lewis and Short " testabilis " means " that has a right to give testimony."

proclamation, that his will and pleasure was that no woman should come into the Theatre before the fifth hower of the day." (Suetonius, *Augustus*, 44, translation of Philemon Holland.)

"To the shew of wrestlers and other champions, he called also the vestall vergins, because at Olympia the priestesses likewise of Ceres, are allowed to see the Games there." (*Ib.*, *Nero*, 12.)

When a Vestal was sick, she was removed from their official residence, and entrusted to the care of some elderly lady of high repute.

Pliny says in his letters :

"I am deeply afflicted at the ill state of health of my friend Fannia, which she contracted during her attendance on Junia, one of the Vestal Virgins. She engaged in this good office at first voluntarily, Junia being her relation ; as she was afterwards appointed to it by an order from the College of Priests ; for these virgins, when any indisposition makes it necessary to remove them from the Temple of Vesta, are always delivered to the care and custody of some venerable matron." (Pliny the Younger, *Epist.*, VII, 19, translation of W. C. Melmoth, 1746.)

In the reign of Valentinian the services of a special physician were also retained when a Vestal was ill. (*Cod. Th.*, XIII, 3, 8.)

The horses of the Vestals carried round their necks metal discs denoting their owners ; of these two have been discovered. The first at the Kircherian Museum is worded as follows : "The property of Calpurnia Prætextata, Lady Superior of the Vestal Virgins" (*Corpus Inscriptionum Latinarum*, Vol. VI, item 2146, p. 598.) Described as lamina ænea (brass plate).

The other runs thus : "Flaviæ Publicæ V. V. Maximæ Immunis in iugo." (Reference as above, item 2147). "Tabella ænea Romæ eruta anno 1748 apud presulem Joannem Bottarium Vaticanæ Bibliothecæ præfectum." A brass tablet dug up at Rome in 1748 in the presence of John Bottarius, prefect of the Vatican Library.

STATUE DRAPÉE D'UNE GRANDE MATRONE, DITE AGRIPPINE.

DRESS OF THE VESTALS

IT is noteworthy that the Vestals, to whom an animal living sacrifice was unknown, only wore white vestments in contrast with those of purple or red worn by other branches of the Priesthood. Their shoes also were of white.

As stated previously, their locks were close cropped at the initiation ceremony, but we have no record to show whether the hair was allowed to grow again. Probably not, as they are never represented with flowing locks, though in certain instances the hair appears to be coiled up at the back of the head.

When attending a sacrifice the Vestals had their heads bound with a band (infula) and covered with a hood (suffibulum). They wore a garment next their skin called " tunica interior," or " interula," or, later on, "subucula." (Horace, *Sat.*, I, 2, 132, and Apuleius, *Florida*, IX, *Met.* VIII, 27.) Over this they wore the stola of the matrons, a long-sleeved woollen tunic with a purple-bordered flounce (instita) to the ankles and covered with the palla.

The palla, the outdoor dress of respectable women, was a large rectangular piece of cloth which could be worn over the stola, like a shawl, usually with the end flung over the left shoulder.

Outside the tunica interula, or chemise, was a cord supporting the breasts, called Strophium (Catullus, LXIV, 65), Mamillare (Martial, XIV, 66).

The statuette, in the Chiaramonti Corridor of the Vatican, found at Hadrian's Villa, represents a Vestal with the fillet binding her hair, with the short palla and the stola down to her ankles. This agrees in detail

53

with the statue, which is in the same gallery, representing the Vestal Tuccia carrying a sieve.

But the finest statue in the same collection, formerly the property of the Mattei family, of the time of Augustus, is that of a Vestal carrying the sacred flame, by means of torches, to a sacrifice.

The infula binds her hair ; the tunica with the palla over it is kept in place by the mamillare cord ; the ends of the stola are gathered up over her arms to allow her action to be free as she proceeds on her mission. Dignity, vivacity, and grace are wonderfully expressed in this work.

The High Vestal, or Lady Superior, always had her head covered with a hood—suffibulum (Varro, *L.L.*, 6, 21)—forming a tippet, which was drawn round over the shoulders, thus forming a hood and tippet in one. (See statues.) It could be worn open or fastened at the neck with a brooch. The suffibulum was a white vestment edged with purple, oblong in shape (a double cube), which all Vestal Virgins were accustomed to have on their heads whenever sacrificing ; and it was held together with a brooch. (Festus, *Ep.*, 349.)

The six Vestals are so represented on the coin of Julia Domna (p. 153), but the High Vestal always wore it as a distinguishing emblem of her office. The best illustration of this is the statue of the High Vestal Prætextata Crassa (A.D. 190–201), found in the Atrium Vestæ, and placed in a cabinet in the National Museum.

The vitta (fillet), infula (band), suffibulum (veil and tippet), fibula (brooch), tunica (shift), stola (robe), strophium (girdle), mamillare or cord, are all distinctly shown.

Several statues of High Vestals were found in the excavations, but only three others with their heads on, Flavia Publicia, the National Museum ; Terentia Flavola, in the Atrium Vestæ ; and Numisia Maximilla, also in the Atrium. These three differ from Crassa's in the tippet not being buckled.

A relief, found by the brothers Chillino at Lecce, in December, 1897, represents the High Vestal with stola

STATUE OF HESTIA (VESTA)
From the Conservatori Palace Museum.
(By permission of Dr. Forbes.)

and suffibulum, and a Vestal in stola, without the
suffibulum, approaching the sacred fire, which is burning on the ground. There exists a statue of Vesta
herself in the Torlonia Museum, formerly the property
of the Justiniana, representing her vested in the
suffibulum, palla and stola. A copy of this, minus the
head, was found in the excavations on the east side of
the Colosseum in 1896, and thence transferred to the
Municipal Museum on the Cœlian, but is now in the
Conservatori palace. The head has since been found
and restored.

VITTA ET INFULA

IT must be realised that there was a great difference between the " Vitta " and the " Infula," although the two are sometimes confused.

The vitta was a simple fillet used for binding the hair to keep it tidy and from off the forehead. Maidens wore one band ; matrons, two. This is illustrated in the case of the Vestals in the three statues in the Vatican, and in the gem of Tuccia (p. 69) and the Lecce relief ; also, in the case of the High Vestals, in the National Museum of Rome.

The infula was a band of white wool wound several times round the head, and worn by the Vestals when performing their ceremonies.

" The infulæ are strands of wool with which the priests' and victims' temples are covered." (Festus, *Ep.*, 113.)

" Whilst, notwithstanding, the twisted band bound their stray plaits." (Prudentius, *Cont. Sym.*, II, 1086.)

As regards the Vestals, the infula is distinctly shown as binding the plaits of hair on the heads of the Virgins, in the National Museum at Rome, the dressing of their hair being exactly alike. The number of the folds seems to have been optional, for it varies in the existing heads.

A relief of a young Vestal's head shows four only ; the statue of the V.V.M., Flavia Publicia, who ruled the order from A.D. 257–283, also shows four folds, as well as the fillet and hair in front.

The head, which we believe to be that of Cœlia Claudiana, who ruled for over thirty years, A.D. 227–57, has four faint folds, but the ends show three only. The front is arranged differently from the others, being made to come to a point above the centre of the forehead, like a diadem, similar to the coins of the heads of Julia Mamæa, the mother, and Orbiana, the wife of Alexander Severus (A.D. 222–36.)

The medallion of the Vestal Bellicia Modesta shows five folds, as does the head of the V.V.M., Numisia Maximilla (A.D. 201–9), in the house of the Vestals. The stern and dignified Prætextata Crassa (A.D. 180–200) in the National Museum shows the vitta and an infula of five folds.

The bust of the Vestal Terentia Flavola, in the National Museum, when she was about twenty-six years of age, shows the three plaits of her hair and the band in six folds. The statue of the same when High Vestal (A.D. 210–15), in the Atrium Vestæ, also has six folds ; so also have two heads in the cabinet of the National Museum of Rome.

It is obvious that the folds of the infula do not represent the " sex crines " or six plaits of hair of brides, for on some the crines can be seen as well as the folds, and the number of the folds vary. Neither could they represent decades of service or rule, for one would thus have served forty years, and the other, in the Hall of Vestals, sixty years, whilst the head represents a virgin of about twenty-six.

I believe, therefore, that there is no signification in the number of the folds.

The word " infula " is sometimes used by poets for " vitta."

" Whose virgin's fillet at the same time bound her hair." (Lucretius, *De Rer. Nat.*, I, 87.)

Priests wore both vitta and infula.

" His brow with sacred fillet wreathed,
His limbs in dazzling armour sheathed."

(Conington's transl., Virgil, *Æneid*, X, 538.)

The animal about to be sacrificed also was adorned with them :

> " Whilst the fleecy infula is bordered by the snow-white fillet." (*Georg.*, III, 487.)

The Vestals wore three kinds of foot coverings : (*a*) the ordinary solea, or sandal, examples of which can be seen in the statues in the Atrium Vestæ ; (*b*) the calceus, or shoe, a capital illustration of which exists in the seated statue of a girl in the new Capitoline Museum ; (*c*) the mitten-shoe, with a place for the big toe (like gloves), as worn by the Japanese ladies. The statues of Numisia Maximilla and Terentia Flavola in the Atrium Vestæ illustrate this.

Their foot-coverings were always white, made from the skin of sacrificial animals.

THE DISCIPLINE OF THE VESTALS

IN view of the high reverence with which the Vestal Virgins were regarded in the religious life of Rome, it is natural to find that the penalties imposed on those who were careless in the performance of their duties, or unfaithful to their vows of chastity, should have been extremely severe.

This attitude of mind was not a matter of a rigid moral code, but was due to a superstitious fear of the vengeance of the God to whom alone the Vestal Virgins belonged, body and soul.

During the thousand years of their existence, we have records only of twenty-two who were alleged to have been false to their vows.

Of these, eighteen were put to death in the prescribed manner, two committed suicide, one was seduced by Nero, and there is no record of her punishment, whilst the remaining one became the Empress of Heliogabalus and died A.D. 225.

Plutarch gives a full account of the disciplinary action taken in the case of unfaithful Vestals in the following passage :

" The Pontifex Maximus, the chief of the Priests, is interpreter of all sacred rites, or rather a superintendent of religion, having the care not only of public sacrifices, but even of private rites and offerings, forbidding the people to depart from the sacred ceremonies, and teaching them how to honour and propitiate the gods. He also has the inspection of the holy virgins called Vestals."

" For smaller offences, these virgins were punished with stripes ; and sometimes the Pontifex Maximus gave them the discipline naked, in some dark place and under cover of a veil ; but she that broke her vow of chastity was buried alive by the Colline Gate.[1]

There, within the walls is raised a little mount of earth, called in Latin ' Agger,' under which is prepared a small cell, with steps to descend it.

In this, are placed a bed, a lighted lamp, and some slight provisions, such as bread, water, milk, and oil, as they thought it impious to take off a person consecrated with the most awful ceremonies, by such a death as that of famine.

The criminal is carried to punishment through the Forum, in a litter well covered without, and bound up in such a manner that her cries cannot be heard. The people silently make way for the litter, and follow it with marks of extreme sorrow and dejection.

There is no spectacle more dreadful than this, nor any day which the city passes in a more melancholy manner.

When the litter comes to the place appointed, the officers loose the cords, the high-priest, with hands lifted up towards heaven, offers some private prayers just before the fatal minute, then takes out the prisoner, who is covered with a veil, and places her upon the steps which lead down to the cell ; after this he retires with the rest of the priests, and when she is gone down, the steps are taken away, and the cell is covered with earth; so that the place is made level with the rest of the mount." (Plutarch, *Numa*, Langhorne's translation.)

It should be noted that the Pontifex Maximus had the power of punishing the Vestal Virgins for disciplinary offences, without consulting the Sacred College.

In the case of any alleged offence against chastity, it was necessary for the whole Sacred College to assemble.

" What is there in all Rome," asks Plutarch in another passage, " so sacred and venerable as the Vestal Virgins, to whose care alone the preservation of the eternal fire is committed ?

[1] The remains of the Colline Gate were found in building the Ministry of Finance in the Via Venti Settembre.

Yet, if their chastity be violated and their reputation stained, they are buried alive ; for when they presume to commit any offence against their gods, they instantly lose that veneration which they claimed as attendants in their service." (Plutarch, *Tib. Gracchus*, anonymous translation, published by Tonson, 1683.)

The reason for the severe treatment of unfaithful Vestals is discussed by Plutarch :

" What is the reason that the Romans punish the holy Vestall Virgins (who have suffered their bodies to be abused and defiled), by no other meanes, than by interring them quicke under the ground.

Is this the cause, for that the manner is to burne the bodies of them that be dead ; and to burie (by the meanes of fire), their bodies who have not devoutly and religiously kept or preserved the divine fire, seemed not just nor reasonable ?

Or haply, because they thought it was not lawful to kill any person who had been consecrated with the most holy and religious ceremonies in the world ; nor to lay violent hands upon a woman consecrated ; and therefore they devised this invention of suffering them to die of their owne selves ; namely to let them downe into a little vaulted chamber under the earth, where they left with them a lampe burning, and some bread, with a little water and milke ; and having so done, cast earth and covered them aloft. And yet for all this, can they not be exempt from a superstitious feare of them thus interred. For even to this day, the priests going over this place, performe (I know not what) anniversary services and rites, for to appease and pacifie their ghosts." (Plutarch, *Romane Questions*, XCVI. Translation by Philemon Holland.)

The historians of Rome furnish us with numerous instances of erring Vestals, their crimes and punishments, a few of which are recorded in the following pages. These incidents were, for religious reasons, treated very seriously, and it is worth noting that Livy often interrupts the sequence of his history to record cases.

It appears that the unfaithful virgins were originally whipped to death, and this was the fate of Ilia or Rhea Silvia of Alba Longa. This was changed in Rome.

" Now the Pontifical law ordains that she shall be buried alive." (Dionysius, I, 78, Spelman's trans., 1758.)

" Tarquin seems to have first instituted the punishments which are inflicted by the Pontiffs on those virgins who do not preserve their virginity. For in his reign, a priestess, by name Pinaria, the daughter of Publius, was discovered to have approached the altars with impurity." (*Ib.*, III, 67.)

" The Pontiffs were informed that one of the Vestals, who preserved the holy fire, by name, Opimia, had lost her virginity, and polluted the holy rites. The Pontiffs, having by tortures, and other proofs, found the information to be true, took from her head the fillets, and, conducting her through the Forum, buried her alive within the walls of the city, and, causing the two men who had debauched her to be scourged and put to death." (*Ib.*, VIII, 89.)

" Lucius Pinarius and Publius Furius were created consuls in 471 B.C. Information was given to the Pontiffs by a slave that one of the Vestal Virgins, who have the care of the perpetual fire, by name Urbinia, had lost her virginity, and, though impure, performed the public sacrifices.

Then the Pontiffs, having removed her from the ministry, brought her to trial ; and, after she was convicted, they ordered her to be whipped with rods, to be carried through the city, and buried alive. One of the two men, who had been the accomplices of her crime, killed himself ; the other, the Pontiffs seized, and ordered him to be scourged in the Forum like a slave, and then put to death." (*Ib.*, IX, 40.)

" In the year 337 B.C. Minucia, a Vestal, who was first of all regarded with suspicion on account of her dress, daintier than was proper, and afterwards on the information of a slave, was accused before the Priests.

After she had by their edict been ordered to absent herself from ritual service and to keep her household available as witnesses, she was, as the outcome of their decision, buried alive beneath the earth in the Field of Sin (Scelerato Campo) by the Colline Gate on the right hand of the metalled road. That name, I believe, was given to that place from the incest." (Livy, VIII, 15.)

That very perfect blackguard, Catiline, had in his earliest youth seduced a Vestal Virgin, besides other offences of the same kind against the laws of God and man. (Sallust, *Cat.*, XV, 1.)

Fabia, a Vestal Virgin, sister-in-law of Cicero's wife, Terentia, was tried for such an offence with Catiline, but was acquitted. (73 B.C., Asconius on Cicero, *De Tog. Cand.*, p. 82, Kiessl.)

Plutarch (*Cato Minor*, VII, 3) speaks of the same lady being in danger of conviction, but in this case it was the equally notorious Clodius who had been calumniating priests and priestesses to the public. It was perhaps in connection with this trouble that Cicero wrote to Terentia how he had wept at hearing how she (Terentia) had been taken away from the Temple of Vesta 58 B.C. (*ad Divers*, XIV, 2, 2). The last phase was when Cicero, addressing the Senate on Catiline's conspiracy 63 B.C. (*in Cat.* IV, 12), described his horror at picturing the headlong flight of matrons, girls, boys and Vestals before the advancing troops of Catiline.

It should be noted that the word incest above (incestus or incestum) is used in a special sense in the case of Vestals, applying to any case of violation of the vow of chastity, no matter with whom.

There was an ancient law, attributed to Tullus Hostilius (see Tacitus, *Annals*, XII, 8), which prescribed a sacrifice of expiation, to be made by the Pontiffs in the Grove of Diana, when incest was committed.

As such intercourse was believed to be unproductive, the propitiation was naturally made to avert the wrath of Diana, the goddess of fertility.

It must of course be realised, as previously stated,

that the reproduction of species, whether human, animal or vegetable, became a religion amongst primitive peoples because it was a necessity in the struggle for existence.

The Divine Command, " Be fruitful and multiply " (Genesis viii. 17), given to Noah, was the Law of the Infant Nations.

The Church of Rome uses the word in a similar sense, i.e., there is spiritual incest between persons related by spiritual affinity or with a person under a vow of chastity. Sir Thomas More says (Confut. Tindale ; works, 361–1) :

"Mayster Martine Luther hymself . . . toke out of religion, a spouse of Christ, liveth with her openly in shameful incest and abhominable bycherie." (*Murray's Dict.*)

Plutarch, in another place, writes :

" What is the cause that the Romanes (having information given unto them, that the Bletonnesians, a barbarous nation, had sacrificed unto their gods a man), sent for the Bletonnesian magistrates peremptorily, as intending to punish them : but after they once understood, that they had so done according to an ancient law of their countrey, they let them go againe without any hurt done unto them : charging them onely, that from thence foorth they should not obey such a law ; and yet they themselves, not many yeeres before, had caused for to be buried quicke in the place, called the Beast Market, two men and two women, that is to say two Greeks, and two Gallo-Greekes or Galatians ? For this seemeth to be verie absurd, that they themselves should do those things, which they reprooved in others as damnable.

May it not be that they judged it an execrable superstition, to sacrifice a man or woman unto the gods, but unto divels they held it necessarie ? Or was it not for that they thought these people who did it by a law or custome, offended lightly, but they themselves were directed thereto by expresse commaundement out of the bookes of Sibylla.

For reported it is, that one of their votaries or Vestall Nunnes named Helbia, riding on horse-back, was smitten by a thunderbolt or blast of lightning : and that the horse was found lying all bare bellied, and herselfe likewise naked, with her smocke and petticote turned up, as if she had done it of purpose : her shooes, her rings, her coife and her head attire cast here and there apart from other things, and withall lilling the toong out of her head.

This strange occurrent, the soothsayers out of their learning interpreted to signifie, that some great shame did betide the sacred virgins, that should be divulged and notoriously knowen : yea, and that the same infamie should reach also as far, as unto some of the degree of gentleman or knights of Rome. Upon this there was a servant belonging unto a certeine Barbarian horseman, who detected three Vestal Virgins to have at one time, forfeited their honour and been naught of their bodies, to wit, Aemilia, Licinia, and Martia, and that they had companied too familiarly with men a long time ; and one of their names was Eutetius, a Barbarian knight and master to the said Enformer. So these Vestall Votaries were punished after they had been convicted by order of law, and found guiltie ; but after that this seemed a fearfull and horrible accident, ordeined it was by the Senate, that the priests should peruse over the bookes of the Sibylla's prophesies, wherein were found (by report), those very oracles which announced and foretold this strange occurrent, and that it portended some great losse and calamitie unto the commonwealth : for the avoiding and diverting whereof, they gave commaundement to abandon unto (I know not what) maligne and divelish strange spirits, two Greekes and two Galatians likewise : and so by burying them quicke in that verie place, to procure propitiation at God's hands." (Plutarch, *Romane Questions*, LXXXIII, translation by Philemon Holland.)

The religious terror caused by a lapse on the part of a Vestal Virgin, is also shewn by the following incident

E

after Hannibal's crushing defeat of the Romans at Cannæ.

Whilst making full allowance for the hysteria that inevitably takes possession of a defeated people, ancient or modern, the occurrence is significant.

Two Vestals had been found guilty of adultery, and one of them was buried alive according to custom, at the Colline Gate, the other taking refuge in suicide.[1]

A clerk of the Chief Priest who had seduced one of these Vestals, was scourged to death by the Pontifex Maximus himself. Then, since the whole affair was regarded as a " prodigium," the Sacred Books were consulted and a special embassy was despatched to the oracle at Delphi with Fabius Pictor as leader. (Livy, XXII, 57.)

Livy also tells us (Book XXI, 62), that in the winter of 218–17 B.C. (when Hannibal was in winter quarters in Northern Italy after the victory of the Trebbia), there was a great religious revival in Rome.

The old saw, " When the Devil was sick," seems to have been as true in ancient as in modern times !

Livy (IV, 44) relates the case of the Vestal Postumia. Here is Philemon Holland's happy translation :

" The same yeare, Posthuma, a Vestall nun, was called in question for incontinence and incest and came to her answere.

A virgin guiltless for any deede done ; but scarcely of good name and fame ; by reason that she was suspected for her apparall and going more light and garish in her attire ; yea, and for her wit, more conceited and pleasant than became a maiden, and nothing respective of the speech of the world.

Her triall was put over to a further day, and she (after she had twice pleaded), in the ende was acquit ; onely the High Priest by the advise and in the name of the whole College, schooled her, and gave her warning to leave her sports, taunts and merry conceits ; and in her raiment to be seene not so deft as devout, and weare her garments rather sainctly than sightly."

---

[1] Floronia and Opimia, 216 B.C.

This is a delightful sidelight on the problem of the eternal feminine.   " Plus ça change, plus c'est la même chose."   One can almost see this very human little sinner, coquettish and perhaps pert, before the " most potent, grave and reverend signiors " of the College of Priests, pleading to cold hypnotic eyes that her only fault was being very much a woman.

There is a case (related also by Livy), during the second Punic War, of a Vestal Virgin being punished by the Pontifex Maximus for allowing the sacred fire to go out.   At this time there was a panic in Rome.

"But of all the wonderous signes, either reported from abroad or seene at home, the minds of men were put in feare for the going out of the fire in the chappell of Vesta.

For which cause, the Vestall Virgin who had the charge that night to looke unto it, was by the com-mandment of P. Licinius, the Bishop (i.e., the Pontifex Maximus), well and thoroughly skourged.   And albeit this hapned by humane negligence, and that the gods portended nothing thereby, yet it was thought good, that an expiation thereof, should be made with greater sacrifices, and a solemne supplication held in the chappell of Vesta." (Livy, XXVIII, 11, translated by Philemon Holland.)

Valerius Maximus (I, I, 7) and Dionysius (II, 68) cite the case of Æmilia, a High Vestal Virgin who was able, miraculously to re-kindle the sacred fire which a negligent novice had allowed to expire.   The story is told as follows (Dion., l.c.) :

"Upon this, they say that Aemilia, who was innocent but distracted at what had happened, stretched out her hands to the altar, and in the presence of the priests, and the rest of the Virgins, said, ' O, Vesta, tutelary goddess of this city, if, during the space of over thirty years, I have performed the holy cere-monies to thee, with purity and justice, and have preserved a pure mind and a chaste body, appear in my defence, and assist me ; and do not suffer your priestess to die the most miserable of all deaths.   But if I have been guilty of any impiety, let my punishment expiate the guilt of the city.' Having said this, she tore off a piece of the linen garment she was wearing, and threw it upon the altar, when, from the ashes long cold, a great flame shone forth."

There is a further interesting reference in Herodian, to an appeal for Divine intervention by a Vestal Virgin, who claimed to be wrongfully accused of infidelity.

Incidentally, the story of the origin of the " Magna Mater " and her arrival in Rome, are given at the same time. The following is an early translation :

" They say that her image (Magna Mater) was let fall by Jove, and that it is unknowne who made it, or what it is made of ; and they firmely beleeve that it is no humane Handiworke. The Tradition is, that it fell in old time from Heaven into a Field of Phrygia, called Pessinus, by occasion of that fall of the Image. . . .

In this Pessinus, the Phrygians in old time, celebrated their Orgia upon the banks of the River Gallus (whence the gelded Priests of the Goddesse are called Galli).

But when the Roman State beganne to flourish, the Oracle telling them that their Empire should continue and overtop all others, if they could get among them the Godesse of Pessinus, they despatched Embassadore into Phrygia, to desire the Goddesses' Image, which was easily granted them, because they alleaged that they were their Cousins of the whole bloud, and descended of Æneas the Phrygian.

When the Image (Magna Mater) was brought by Ship to the mouth of Tyber (which was then the only port the Romans had), suddenly by some divine power, the Ship stood still, and could not be moved with all the haling and pulling of the Romans.

At last, a Vestall Nun, that was falsely accused to have lost her virginity (which she had vowed to keepe inviolate) fearing she should be condemned, besought the People to make the Goddesse Pessinuntia her judge ; which being admitted, shee untied her girdle, and praied in the hearing of all, that if the

THE VESTAL TUCCIA

Copied from an ancient gem. (Montfauçon.)

Goddesse knew her to be a Virgin immaculate, she would command the Ship to remove.

Then, tying her girdle to the Ship, she pulled and it followed her ; the Romans admitting both the Divinity of the Goddesse, and Virginity of the Priest-esse. And thus much of the story of the Goddesse Pessinuntia, which though it be somewhat long, yet I trust will not be unpleasing to them that are not versed in Roman Antiquities." (Herodian, I, 11, interpreted out of the Greek Original, 1629.)

Suetonius (*Tib.*, II) refers to this same virgin, Claudia, " Shee that drew forth the ship with the sacred images of the Idaean Mother of the Gods stick-ing fast and grounded within the shalows of Tiberis, having before made her praier openly. That as she was a true and pure virgin, so the ship might follow her, and not otherwise." (Trans. by Philemon Holland.)

This case has attracted the notice even of Saint Augustine. In enumerating Pagan miracles, he refers to this and another incident :

" The drawing on of the ship that brought Bere-cynthiades' statue from Phrygia (being otherwise not to be moved by huge strength of men and beasts) by one woman with her girdle, in testimony of her chastity ; and the carrying of water from Tyber in a sieve by a Vestal (Tuccia), thereby acquitting herself from an accusation of adultery." (*De Civitate Dei*, Book X, Chap. 16, translated by T. Healey, 1620.)

Added to this are notes, probably by Healey :

" The ship that came from Pessinum with the Mother of the gods sticking immoveably in Tyber, on ground, Q. Claudia, a Vestall (slandered from in-continency because she loved to go handsome) tooke her girdle and knitting it to the ship, praied Bere-cynthia, if she knew her chaste, to follow her, and so she did. Whereupon, Claudia had a statue set up before the Goddesse temple, that stood safe when the temple was twise burned."

NOTE.—This incident is depicted in a relief on an altar in the Capitoline Museum.

THE VESTALS DURING THE EMPIRE

DURING the time of the Republic and of the earlier part of the Empire, the status of the Vestals remained unchanged.

During the reigns of such abnormal Emperors as Nero, Commodus and Heliogabalus, the Vestals and their charges, the holy relics, had unpleasant adventures, but till the conversion of Constantine to Christianity (A.D. 313) their position was in no way weakened or even threatened, and even under Constantine and his Christian successors, the Vestal Establishment showed a remarkable tenacity of life.[1]

Under Augustus the status of the Vestal Virgins received serious imperial attention.

Suetonius (*Augustus*, XXXI, translated) writes :

" He increased both the number and dignity of the priests and their emoluments especially of the Vestal Virgins. And when it was imperative that a fresh virgin should be selected in place of one who had died, and many men were canvassing in order not to have to offer their daughters to the drawing of lots, he gave a solemn assurance that if the age of any one of his own nieces were that prescribed, he would have offered her.

He also revived certain of the ancient ceremonies which had gradually fallen into disuse, as well as the auguries for general supplications by the Flamen Dialis, the rites of the Lupercalia and the Century and Cross-road Games. . . .

He forbade those who had not reached man's age to compete at the Lupercalia." (See Appendix II.)

---

[1] In the case of the establishment at Alba, the Sacred Fire was actually kept burning until the end of the fourth century A.D.

As one would expect, the Vestal Virgins in the reign of Nero (A.D. 54–68) were not an object of reverence.

Suetonius (*Nero*, 28) tells us that the Emperor violated a Vestal Virgin named Rubria, and further that he summoned " to the show of wrestlers and other champions also the Vestal Virgins, because at Olympia, the Priestesses likewise of Ceres are allowed to see the Games there." (Suetonius, *Nero*, 12.)

Under Domitian (A.D. 81), Pliny the Younger places on record the vindictiveness of that dissolute ruler towards the Lady Superior of the Vestals. He writes :

" For Domitian was in a very great rage ; and that rage was still encreased by the want of sufficient eveidence to support that horrible sentence he was determined to give.

And when the Emperor resolved that Cornelia, chief of the Vestal Virgins, should be buried alive, as thinking to make his reign illustrious by such an example, he summoned by authority as High Priest, or rather by his tyrannic disposition, and the wantonness of an absolute prince, the chief priests to meet together, not in the Pontifical College, but at his country seat at Alba, where with a crime equal to that, which he seemed to punish, without citing her to appear, or giving her leave to speak in her own defence, he condemned her of incest ; although he himself had not only been guilty of the same crime with his brother's daughter, but had also been the occasion of her death : for she died of abortion in her widowhood.

The chief priests were immediately sent to see the sentence against Cornelia put into execution. She, at one time invoking Vesta, and then appealing to the rest of the gods, among other exclamations, frequently repeated this one in particular. ' Cæsar thinks I am guilty of incest. I, who performed the sacred rites when he conquered and triumphed ! '

Whether she meant this by way of flattery or derision is doubtful." (Pliny the Younger, *Ep.*, IV, 11, translation by the Earl of Orrery, 1751. See also Juvenal, IV, 7–10, and Suet., *Dom.*, VIII.)

Herodian has the following record of the ill treatment of the Vestals by Caracalla (A.D. 211–17) :

" He cut off the flower of the nobility and gentry. Then sent he into the provinces and massacred all the presidents and procurators . . . yea, whole nights were spent in such tragicall executions of all sorts of people. He buried the Vestall Virgins quicke, pretending they had lost their virginity." (Herodian, IV, 6, 4, out of the Greeke originall, 1629.)

It was left to that megalomaniac, Heliogabalus (A.D. 218–22), to outstrip all the other Roman Emperors in sacrilege.

Heliogabalus, it should be remembered, had consecrated himself as the true God, and attempted to impose his cult on the Roman world.

Let Lampridius tell the story. He writes :

" But when he (Heliogabalus) first entered the city, neglecting those matters which were in progress in the province, he consecrated Heliogabalus (i.e. himself), on the Palatine hill next to the Imperial Palace and built a temple for him, being anxious to remove into that temple both the image of the Great Mother Cybele, and the fire of Vesta and the Ancilia and all objects of veneration to the Romans, and doing this in order that no god should be worshipped at Rome except Heliogabalus.

He committed incest with a Vestal Virgin.[1] He removed the secret relics and profaned the worship of the Roman People. He wanted to extinguish the eternal fire, nor did he wish to extinguish only the religious beliefs of the Romans, but he aimed at one single object through the whole world, that Heliogabalus should be worshipped everywhere as the only god. And he broke into the inner shrine (penus) of Vesta, which virgins alone and priests alone enter, himself defiled with every moral corruption and in the company of men who had defiled themselves. He tried to carry off the holy relic, and after seizing a sacred jar

---

[1] This refers to Julia Aquilia Severa.

under the impression that it was the real one, though the High Vestal had shewn him a false one and he had found nothing in it, he dashed it down and broke it. And nevertheless, he robbed the worship of nothing, since several are said to have been made like it, in order that no one might be able to steal it." (See Appendix III.)

A further account of this same Emperor's sacrilege is furnished in the following passage from Herodian :

" After pretending hee was in Love, and intending now to shew his manhood, he (Heliogabalus) violently tooke out of Vesta's sacred Nunry at Rome, a Vestall Virgin (who by the Divine Laws was to continue in chastitie and virginitie to her end) and married her. And when he heard that the Senate was much aggrieved at that sacrilegious act, he sent them a consolatory letter ; certifying them ' That it was but a humane sinne ; That he was inchanted with the magicke of her beautie ; and it was no incongruitie, for a priest to marry a priestesse ; which was therefore a most sacred match.' But this wife kept he not long, but cashiering her, took a third, which was said to be of Commodus linage. Nor did he thus play at fast and loose with humane matrimonies ; but now his God also (whose priest hee was) wanted a wife. Hee tooke therefore, into his bed-chamber the image of Pallas, which the Romans kept in secret veneration, unseen of any ; and after that day had never been removed since it was brought from Troy, but only when the Temple was fired ; and so he married that Goddesse and his God together in the palace. Soone after giving out that his God liked not such a martiall wife, that was ever in armes, he commanded the image of Urania to be brought which having beene exceedingly adored by the Carthaginians and Africans, was erected (as they say), by Queene Dido (the Phœnician), what time she reedified Carthage, by cutting an oxehide.[1]

---

[1] The strips of ox-hide were laid out to give the measurements of the city.

This Goddesse, the Africans call Urania ; the Phœnicians Astroarch or the Moone. Antonine (Heliogabalus) said, it would agree bravely to marry the Sunne and Moone together. He therefore sent for the image, and all the treasure and gold in the Temple, giving it to his God for a portion with her. When the image was brought and set neere to Heliogabalus, he commanded all the people of Rome and Italy to use all publike and private Feasts and Exhilarations for joy of the God's wedding." (Herodian, V, 6, interpreted out of the Greeke from the originall, 1629.)

THE END OF THE VESTALS

THE conversion of Constantine to Christianity (Edict of Milan, A.D. 313) did not at once involve that of the mass of his subjects.

The national change of religion was slowly and carefully engineered.[1]

Pagans long remained in an overwhelming majority, even in the civilised parts of the Empire, though the temples were steadily plundered. Eusebius (*Vit. Const.*, Lib. II, *c.* 56–60), implies that idolaters were permitted to offer sacrifices and to practice every part of their worship.

The rate of the change was accelerated by the Emperor's sons, Constans and Constantius (A.D. 360), and Constantius issued a law that temples were immediately to be shut and no sacrifices to be offered ; the severest penalties against offenders being announced.

The law, however, cannot have been enforced long, for the statesman Symmachus, " the last of the Pagans," (A.D. 340–410), says of Constantius :

" That Emperor suffered the privileges of the Vestal Virgins to remain inviolate.

He bestowed the sacerdotal dignities on the nobles of Rome, granted the customary allowance to defray the expenses of the public rites and sacrifices ; and although he had embraced a different religion, he never attempted to deprive the Empire of the sacred worship of antiquity." (Gibbon, chap. 21.)

Julian (A.D. 361–3), called, not altogether fairly, " the Apostate," while he tolerated all religions,

[1] See G. P. Baker, *Constantine the Great and the Christian Revolution*, Gibbon, chaps. XVI and XXV.

restored Paganism to its old position, but under his successors, Jovian (A.D. 363–4), Valentinian and Valens (A.D. 363–78), though there was general toleration, Christianity recovered ground.

It is to be noted that in this reign, in A.D. 364, Cœlia Concordia was the chief Vestal Virgin and a pedestal believed to be hers was found in November, 1883, with the name erased. (See C.I.L., VI., 32422.)

This lady became a Christian, and her last act on leaving the Atrium was to erase her name from the pedestal.

In the garden of Federicus Cæsius in 1591, near the Arch of Gallienus a pedestal and statue to the High Vestal Cœlia Concordia existed as late as 1706, but I do not know what has become of it. (Gruter, CCCX, 1 ; C.I.L., VI, 2145.) It was inscribed thus :

COELIAE. CONCORDIAE. VIR GINI VESTALI. MAXIMAE. FABIA. PAVLINA. C. F. STAT VAM FACIENDAM. CONLO CANDAMQVE CVRAVIT. CVM. PROPTER EGREGIAM. EIVS. PUDICITIAM.   INSIGNEM QVE CIRCA. CVLTVM. DI VINVM SANCTITATEM. TVM. QVOD HAEC. PRIOR. EIVS. VIRO VETTIO. AGORIO. PRAE TEXTATO. V.C. OMNIA. SING- VLARI DIGNOQVE ETIAM. AB HVIVS MODI VIRGINIBVS. ET. SACERDOTIBVS. COLI. STATVAM. COLLOCARAT.

" For Cœlia Concordia, High Vestal Virgin, Fabia Paulina, daughter of Gaius, had this statue made and erected, not only on account of her remarkable purity and her exceptional piety in divine worship, but also because she first had set up a statue to her (i.e. Fabia's) husband, Vettius Agorius Prætextatus, Senator, a man illustrious in all respects and deserving to be honoured by virgins and priests of this class."

The statue of Prætextatus, found in 1883, still stands in the Atrium. His religious activities were remarkable. He was a leading Pagan, Priest of Vesta and the Sun, Augur, " Father of Fathers " in the worship of Mithras and initiate of many mysteries,

THE V.V.M. COELIA CONCORDIA WHO RESIGNED AND
BECAME A CHRISTIAN (A.D. 375)

Sketched by Hemelario 1591.

including those of Eleusis and the Bull (Tauroboliatus), this last involving douching in blood from a new-killed bull. He was governor of Achaia in A.D. 362 and Prefect of Rome in A.D. 368, and as such settled a quarrel between two churchmen, Ursinus and Damasus, for the See of Rome by expelling the former from the city.

The Vestals' wish to erect a statue to him was opposed by Symmachus as an innovation and unbecoming to Vestal modesty (*Ep.*, II, 36). He and his wife, who herself was an initiate of numerous mysteries, including that of the Bull, lived happily united for forty years, and exchanged long and loving inscriptions. (C.I.L., VI, 1779.)

The statue to Cœlia Concordia is described and illustrated by Giovanni Hemelario (*Lipsius in Græv. Thes.*, V, 656) as follows :

" The statue is of white Parian marble, perfectly worked, head, arms, and the extremity of the feet mutilated. She had a necklace adorned with pearls, from which a brooch hung from her shoulders, but that was broken to pieces when the statue was moved. At the back the fillets were apparent ; running down into a knot from the neck or head. The extremities of the hair were not apparent."

When Gratian became Emperor in 375 he refused the title of Pontifex Maximus, and prohibited the pagan religion as a state religion. (Zosimus, IV, 36, *sub fin.*).

I believe that Cœlia Concordia proclaimed herself a Christian, and that is why her name is erased from the pedestal and her head missing from the statue.

In Hemelario's design of the necklace and brooch a cross is distinctly shown in the pendant.

Her name was probably erased by her own order when she joined the living Truth after quenching the fire which for over eleven hundred years represented the light and truth to Rome.

This pedestal is 4 ft. 9$\frac{1}{2}$ in. high, by 2 ft. 4$\frac{1}{2}$ in.

wide. Prudentius mentions (*Peristeph*, II, 528) a Vestal named Claudia who joined the Christian Church.

Still, the Emperors, whatever their own religious views, almost uniformly had conformed to the old religion and held the ancient office of Pontifex Maximus. Gratian, who reigned from A.D. 375 to 383, refused this honour as mentioned. He made a complete clearance of Paganism and even removed from the Senate-house, the ancient statue of Victory. He met with determined opposition and an influential body of Roman nobles, headed by Symmachus, sought an interview in order to protest, but Gratian refused to receive them (382).

After the death of Gratian, another deputation was led by Symmachus to Valentinian II (384), and on this occasion, Ambrose, Archbishop of Milan, debated with him before the Emperor.

An interesting literature of controversy between Symmachus for the Pagans, and Ambrose and Prudentius for the Christians, has come down to us.

A curious passage from the letters of Symmachus (Book X, Ep. 54) is translated by Gibbon (chap. 28).

The City of Rome personified, is pleading the cause of her old religion :

" Most excellent princes," says the venerable matron, " Fathers of your country, pity and respect my age, which has hitherto flowed in an uninterrupted course of piety. Since I do not repent, permit me to continue in the practice of my ancient rites. Since I am born free, permit me to enjoy my domestic institutions. This religion has reduced the world under my laws. These rites have repelled Hannibal from the city and the Gauls from the Capitol. Were my gray hairs reserved for such intolerable disgrace? I am ignorant of the new system, that I am required to adopt ; but I am well assured, that the correction of old age is always an ungrateful and ignominious office."

In the continuation of this passage given below, Symmachus actually attributes public calamities to the change of religion and refers specifically to the abolition of the Vestals.

This petition is also found in the letters of Ambrose (pp. 96 *sqq.* of Pusey's translation of Ambrose's letter in his translation of the Fathers, Ep. XVII).

(Sec. 8.) "He (Constantius) left uncurtailed the privileges of the sacred virgins, he filled the priestly offices with men of noble birth, he allowed the cost of the Roman ceremonies. . . ."

(Sec. 11.) "What advantage accrue to your treasury from the abolition of the privilege of the Vestal Virgins?

Shall that be denied under princes the most munificent, which the most parsimonious have granted? Their sole honour consists in their wages, so to speak, of chastity. As their fillets adorn their heads, so it is esteemed by them an honour to be free to devote themselves to the ministry of sacrifices. It is but the bare name of exemption, i.e. from taxes, which they ask, for their poverty exonerates them from any other payment. So that he who reduces their means, contributes to their praise, for virginity dedicated to the public welfare is meritorious in proportion as it is without reward."

(Sec. 12.) "Far be such gains from the purity of your treasury. The exchequer of good princes should be replenished by the spoils of enemies, not by the losses of ministers of religion."

(Sec. 13.) "The Imperial exchequer retains also lands bequeathed by the will of dying persons to the sacred virgins and priests. I implore you as Priests of Justice, to restore to the sacred functionaries of your city the right of inheriting. . . .

Freedmen may take legacies, slaves are allowed due latitude of bequeathing by will, only the noble virgins and ministers of sacred rites are excluded from inheritance. . . .

(Sec. 14.) The laws of our ancestors provided for

the Vestal Virgins and the ministers of the gods a moderate maintenance and just privileges. This gift was preserved inviolate till the time of degenerate money changers, who diverted the maintenance of sacred chastity into a fund for the payment of base porters.

A public famine ensued on this act and disappointed the hopes of all the provinces."

Anbrose very seriously met Symmachus on his own ground and urged the superior merits of Christian maidens who were not paid a salary.

(Ambrose, Ep. XVIII, p. 104 of Pusey's letters of Ambrose in his translation of the Fathers.)

"Let the Vestal Virgins, he says, enjoy their privileges. It is for those to say this, who cannot believe in gratuitous virginity, it is for them to allure by profit who distrust virtue. But how many virgins have their promised rewards obtained them? They have barely seven Vestals. Such is the whole number whom the veiled and filleted head, the dye of the purple vest, the pompous litter surrounded by attendants, and a prescribed period of virginity have collected."

(Sec. 13.) "Let them turn their mental and bodily eye to us, let them behold a people of chastity, an undefiled multitude, a virgin assembly. No fillets to adorn their heads, but a veil of common use though dignified by chastity, the blandishments of beauty not curiously sought out but cast aside; no purple trappings, no luxurious delicacies, but frequent fastings. . . . That is not a virginity to be bought for money, but preserved for love of holiness; that is not integrity which is bid for at an auction by a pecuniary equivalent, to last but for a time."

I do not wish to prolong unduly extracts from the rival advocates on the general question of the respective merits of Christianity and Paganism, but I would offer, in conclusion, a translation of a curious passage of Prudentius on the belated marriage of a veteran Vestal. It will be remembered that after thirty years of service the Vestal was free to marry, though such marriages seem as a rule to have been not particularly happy.

Prudentius contra Symmachum II. (1064–1099.)

" I will discuss the rules under which the maid who now becomes the pride of Vestal Virginity, wields every charm of modesty. Why, first small girls are taken in their tender years, before the free choice of their own free will, aglow with glory of chastity and love of the gods rejecting the lawful fetters of the sex destined for marriage.

Their captive modesty is bound apprentice before the unwelcome altar and while for the luckless girls there is an end of pleasure from their virginal bodies, their mind is not virginal, nor is any respite found in bed, on which the woman who may not wed, sighs for her secret wound and the marriage torches she has lost.

Then, because her hope still living does not kill her vital fire—for later on she may lawfully kindle her in-effective flames (or ' the torches laid by in store '), and wreathe the merry bridal veil over her thinning white hair ; at the time appointed, Vesta, seeking in vain her unwithered limbs, in the end disdains her aged virginity.

Then ready for wedlock, her vital force may swell, but no love can quicken her for a mother's birth. She weds, an old woman worn with service, when her holy task is accomplished and the hearth is desolate at which her youth did slavery.

She betakes her veteran wrinkles to the marriage couch and there, a new-wed bride in a chilly bed, learns to warm herself.

Meantime, while the looped fillet binds her straying tresses, and as a virgin priestess she kindles the coals of fate, she drives like a public pageant through the crowded streets, leaning back in a cushioned car, and with veiled face, parades herself a virgin for the city to gaze at.

Thence to the throng of the stalls goes her gentle modesty and her piety that knows nought of bloodshed to watch the gory bouts of the men and with her sainted eyes to gaze on butchery and on wounds sold as fodder for slaughter, she sits, for all to see, with the reverend trappings of her fillets and takes her pleasure in the trainers.

Oh for her gentle, tender spirit ! She rises on tip-toe for each stroke and as often as the victor plunges his blade into some throat, she vows that this is her darling pleasure, and shrinking maiden that she is, with thumb turned down, she bids slash open the breast of a prostrate warrior."

Long after the official abolition of the Vestals, it is amazing to find Symmachus writing to the Emperor Valentinian about the unfaithfulness of a Vestal and discussing the penalties to be inflicted exactly in the manner in which he might have written during the Republic. Symmachus was Pontifex Maximus and as such was charged with the discipline of the Vestals.

"Following the precedents of preceding ages, during the prefecture of that most distinguished and honourable man my brother, punishment for unchastity was inflicted by our College on the Vestal Virgin Primigenia who was in charge of the Alban rites.

But since in its letters, reasonable grounds are given why a woman accused of so serious a crime cannot lawfully be admitted within the walls of the Eternal City and why he cannot himself travel to distant places ; since a crime ought to be dealt with where it was committed, we have considered necessary the establishment in the neighbourhood of an authority on which provincial jurisdiction has been conferred in order that the severity always employed in such cases may be visited upon Primigenia who has defiled the mysteries of the state ritual and upon her seducer, who has not denied his offence.

You will therefore deign, after considering the confessions which have revealed the drama of the abominable crime, to avenge by the execution of the guilty persons the peace of mind of a most pure-minded age."

The question arises, who at a date after the official abolition of paganism inflicted the punishment.

The changes made by Gratian cannot entirely have freed Rome from Paganism, for some hundreds of temples were left in operation and Ambrose complains (*Ep.*, XVIII, 33) that the nostrils of Christians were still offended by the savour of sacrifices.

As late as about A.D. 400, Serena, the wife of the great general, Stilicho, and niece of the Emperor Theodosius happened upon a temple of Cybele, served by one Vestal solitary but still sufficiently respected, for the jewellery, which adorned the statue of the goddess, to have escaped plunder.

She took the jewellery and put it on with the consequences related below by Zosimus the historian, another of the surviving Pagans.

Zosimus (Book V, Sec. 138) writes thus of the last Vestal :

" Alaric being already near Rome, and besieging those that were inside the city (408), the Senate suspected Serena (the wife of Stilicho, niece of Theodosius), of having perhaps attracted the barbarians against the city.

The entire Senate, and Claudia, the sister of the prince (Honorius), were unanimous in the opinion that they ought to put Serena to death, because of the present evils ; for if they took from amongst them Serena, Alaric would quickly depart from the city, there not remaining a person from whom he could expect to obtain it.

This suspicion was in reality false, because such treachery had never entered the mind of Serena.

Anyway, she had to pay the penalty of having violated the holy things, as it does me the pleasure to relate here.

When Theodosius the Elder, having defeated the Rebel Eugenius, came to Rome, and created in all people a contempt or neglect of Divine Worship, denying to defray the charge of holy things out of the publick stock, the priests of both sexes were turn'd out and banish'd, and the temples bereft of all their sacrifices.

Whereupon, Serena, scoffing at them, would needs see the temple dedicated to the Mother of the Gods (that is the Temple of Cybele on the Palatine Hill).

In which when she saw certain bracelets and attire about the neck of Rhea's statue suitable to the divine worship which was paid to her, she took it off of the statue and put it about her own neck.

And when a certain old maid, that was the onely person left of all the Vestal Virgins, upbraided her with such a wicked action even to her teeth, she not onely gave her very ill language, but commanded her Attendants to carry or drive her away. But notwithstanding, the old woman, as she was going from the place, pray'd that whatsoever was due to such impiety, might fall upon Serena, her husband and children. But Serena took no notice of what she said, and went out of the temple well pleased with what she had gotten ; though afterward there often appear'd to her something not onely fantastick in a dream, but real, when she was awake, which did foretel her death.

But others too, besides her, saw the like things ; and so far did that just vengeance, which uses to punish the wicked, discharge its duty, that though Serena knew what would happen, she took no care of her self, but submitted that neck about which she had put the Goddesses attire, even to a halter." (Translation 1684, anonymous.)

As Stilicho was afterwards beheaded, and Serena strangled, no doubt the courageous old Vestal felt that her gods were vindicated.

It is to be regretted that Zosimus did not hand us down the name of this gallant priestess of the ancient faith, the last of the Vestal Virgins of Rome.

THE ABOLITION OF THE ORDER

AFTER the Roman religion had run a course of one thousand and more years, Zosimus (IV, 36, *sub. fin.*) tells us that Gratian in 375 refused the office of Pontifex Maximus ; he also abolished the functions of the Vestal Virgins as mentioned above.

In 382 Gratian prohibited their public services, withheld their privileges and state support ; and closed the Temple of Vesta (*Cod. Theod.*, Lib. XVI, tit. 10, 20 ; Ambrose, *Epist.*, XVII, 11, 12).

The ceremonies were finally suppressed by Theodosius in A.D. 394.

" Theodosius directed his attention towards the suppression of idolatry, and issued a law commanding the demolition of idolatrous temples. The Faithful Emperor (Theodosius) abolished these rites, root and branch, and consigned them to eternal oblivion." (Theodoret, *Eccles. Hist.*, V, 21.)

This quarter of the city was finally destroyed by the great fire when Robert Guiscard burned Rome from the Lateran to the Capitol in 1084.

During this long period of nearly seven hundred years the Atrium Vestæ underwent many changes, and received other tenants, for the new excavations show that it had been inhabited after the Vestals were abolished.

Beneath the level of the present Atrium Vestæ exist mosaic floors and walls of the building that occupied this site before the fire of 192. The base of the corner column, behind the first pedestal, rests upon a beautiful mosaic pavement. They occupied the place of others and had themselves to make way for a brighter faith.

At the rear of the first pedestal a terra-cotta jar was discovered containing a brooch bearing the name of

Pope Martin III (943–6) ; a gold coin of Edward, son of Alfred the Great (901–25) ; and 824 Anglo-Saxon silver coins of the above Edward, Edgar Athelstan (925–41), and Edmund I (941–8). We may presume that this money was brought to Rome by some Anglo-Saxon tourist who left his all and fled when the building was finally destroyed by fire ; or that it formed part of a donation of " Peter's Pence."

Ethelwolf, the English king during the time of Leo IV (845–57), was the first British monarch who gave tribute to the See of Rome ; and, as such, his portrait is to be seen in chiaroscuro by Caravaggio, in the Stanze of the Incendio del Borgo in the Vatican. A coin of an Archbishop of Canterbury was also found.

On November 17th, 1899, 397 gold Byzantine coins were found in the first room on the right, south, side, in the trap of a drain :

The details of these coins were as follows :

1.	Flavius Julius Constantine II (337–61).
7.	Valentinianus III (425–55).
8.	Marcianus (450–7).
10.	Elia Marcia Eufemia, his daughter, wife of Anthemius.
24.	Leo I, Isaurian (457–74).
2.	Libius Severus (461–5).
345.	Anthemius (467–72).

ANALOGOUS ESTABLISHMENTS IN
OTHER COUNTRIES

WHEN one comes to consider the Establishments in other countries and ages, similar to that of the Vestal Virgins at Rome, one is amazed at their number and the degree of resemblance.

Everywhere from Ireland to Peru, from the Blackfoot Indian of America to the Hereros of South Africa, almost identical cults are to be found, of which the common basic idea is the worship of the Sun God or the Fire-God, with Virgins as priestesses of the God's holy rites.

These resemblances, which at first seem remarkable, become upon reflection perfectly natural.

They spring in every case from fundamental emotions, fear and reverence for the Sun, and the Lightning which probably gave the first fire to mankind.

To the primitive mind it was inevitable that these greatest forces of Nature, life-giving, benevolent, and cleansing, should be deified, and as a necessary corollary, worshipped and served.

The Blackfoot Indians of North America used to worship the Sun as their principal god, and four days before the August new moon the High Priest halted the tribe on the march, suspended all hunting and made the people fast, and take vapour baths.

A virgin was then chosen from the tribe, to represent the Moon, and be the bride of the Sun.

Amongst the other duties she was obliged to maintain a sacred fire of fragrant herbs.

The analogies between the rites of the Hereros of South-West Africa and those of ancient Rome are remarkable.

The Vestal Fire of Rome, as previously shown, was

undoubtedly a survival of the King's Hearth, and in South-West Africa, the sacred fire burns day and night in the hut of the Herero chief.

If it is at any time extinguished, this is regarded as an evil omen, as in Rome, to be expiated by sacrifices, and the means of renewing the fire was in both cases identical.

The Roman fire was fed from the sacred oak tree ; the fire of the Hereros must also be fed from a tree that is sacred to the tribe.

Beside the sacred fire, the images of the Ancestors must be kept, the Lares of Rome, and the Ozondume of the Hereros.

The sacred fire of the Hereros must be tended by the virgin daughter of the chief, and this was undoubtedly the case in the beginnings of the worship of Vesta in Rome.

The Hereros of South-West Africa have also certain priestly rites having as their object the prosperity and multiplication of the cattle. This finds a parallel in the festival of the Parilia in ancient Rome. But the parallels which are of the greatest interest are found in the cases of the Nuns of St. Bridget in Ireland, the Virgins of the Sun in Peru, and Hestia of Greece.

The first two of these may be noted in the following passages from Giraldus of Cambrai, and Prescott's famous *History of the Conquest of Peru* :

Giraldus Cambrensis writes in the twelfth century as follows :

" In Kildare of Leinster, which the glorious Bridget made illustrious, there are many wonders worthy of mention. Foremost amongst these is the Fire of Bridget, which they call inextinguishable, not that it cannot be extinguished, but because the nuns and holy women so anxiously and accurately cherish and nurse the fire, that during so many centuries from the time of the Virgin it has ever remained unextinguished and the ashes have never accumulated, although in so long a time so vast a pile of wood hath here been consumed.

Whereas in the time of Bridget twenty nuns here served the Lord, she herself being the Twentieth, there have been only nineteen from the time of her glorious departure, and they have not added to their number.

But as each nun in her turn tends the fire for one night, when the twentieth night comes, the last virgin, having placed the wood ready, saith :

'Bridget, tend that fire of thine, for this is Thy night.'

And the fire being so left, in the morning they find it unextinguished, and the fuel consumed in the usual way.

That fire is surrounded by a circular hedge of bushes, within which a male does not enter, and if he should presume to enter as some rash men have attempted, he does not escape divine vengeance."

St. Bridget was Abbess of Kildare in the sixth century, and tradition has it that it was to her St. Bride's in Fleet Street was dedicated. Her fame spread far beyond Ireland.

It was she who hung her cloak on a sunbeam, though St. Dunstan, the other patron saint of Fleet Street, performed a yet more remarkable feat, for his chasuble hung itself suspended in the air without so much as a sunbeam for a help !

Henry of London, Archbishop of Dublin in the twelfth century, extinguished the fire, but it was relit and continued burning until the suppression of the monasteries in the reign of Henry VIII.

Adjoining the church at Kildare you are shown to-day the fire house where St. Bridget is said to have lit the sacred flame, but as it is a stone cellar, the probability of its being the actual place is remote.[1]

St. Bridget was regarded as the Patron Saint, or what in earlier days would be called the Goddess of Poets, Doctors and Smiths.

It is probable that her nuns, called Inghean na

[1] *Fleet Street in Seven Centuries,* by Walter George Bell (Chap. XVIII).

Dagna—"daughters of fire"—were the successors to some Celtic order of Vestals, and we know that there were female Druids.

As stated by Giraldus Cambrensis, the fire was made in a circular place, as at Rome, and the nuns were permitted to fan it or stimulate it with bellows, but not with the human breath.

As a matter of fact, the custom of maintaining a perpetual fire was not confined to Kildare, but there are records of similar fires being maintained in numerous monasteries, where a special oratory was dedicated to this purpose, notably at Kilmainham in Dublin, better known in modern times as the County Jail.

VIRGINS OF THE SUN AMONG THE INCAS OF PERU

" ANOTHER singular analogy with Roman Catholic Institutions is presented by the Virgins of the Sun, the 'elect,' as they were called, to whom I have already had occasion to refer.

These were young maidens dedicated to the service of the deity, who, at a tender age, were taken from their homes and introduced into convents, where they were placed under the care of certain elderly matrons, 'mamaconas,' who had grown gray within their walls.

Under these venerable guides, the holy virgins were instructed in the nature of their religious duties.

Besides the duty of watching over the Sacred Fire, they had to bake the cakes offered to the Sun at his great festivals, and to brew the wine which the Inca and his family drank on these occasions.

They were employed in spinning and embroidery, and with the fine hair of the vicuna, wove the hangings for the temples and the apparel for the Inca and his household.

It was their duty above all, to watch over the Sacred Fire obtained at the festival of Raymi.

From the moment they entered the establishment, they were cut off from all connection with the world, even with their own family and friends. No one but the Inca and the Coya, or queen, might enter the consecrated precincts.

The greatest attention was paid to their morals, and visitors were sent every year to inspect the institutions and to report on the state of their discipline.

Woe to the unhappy maiden who was detected in an intrigue !

By the stern law of the Incas, she was to be buried

alive, her lover was to be strangled, and the town or village to which he belonged was to be razed to the ground and ' sowed with stones' as if to efface every memorial of his existence.

One is astonished to find so close a resemblance between the institutions of the American Indian and the ancient Roman rites.

Chastity and purity of life are virtues in women, that would seem to be of equal estimation with the barbarian and with the civilised ; yet the ultimate destination of the inmates of these religious houses was materially different.

The great establishment at Cuzco consisted wholly of maidens of the royal blood, who amounted, it is said, to no less than fifteen hundred.

The provincial convents were supplied from the daughters of the curacas and inferior nobles, and occasionally, when a girl was recommended by great personal attractions, from the lower classes of the people.

The ' Houses of the Virgins of the Sun ' consisted of low ranges of stone buildings, covering a large extent of ground, surrounded by high walls, which excluded those within entirely from observation.

They were provided with every accommodation for the fair inmates, and were embellished in the same sumptuous and costly manner as the palaces of the Incas and the temples ; for they received the particular care of government, as an important part of the religious establishment.

All the furniture of the convents down to the pots, pans and jars, was of gold and silver, just as in the Temple of the Sun.

In this respect, they differed vastly from the Vestals of Rome whose religious utensils were always of plain earthenware even in the most luxurious days of Rome.

" Yet the career of all the inhabitants of these cloisters was not confined within their narrow walls. Though Virgins of the Sun, they were brides of the Inca, and at a marriageable age, the most beautiful among them were selected for the honours of his bed, and transferred to the royal seraglio. The full complement of this amounted in time, not only to hundreds, but thousands, who all found accommodations in different palaces throughout the country. When the monarch was disposed to lessen the number of his establishment, the concubine with whose society he was willing to dispense, returned, not to her former monastic residence, but to her own home ; where, however humble might be her original condition, she was maintained in great state, and far from being dishonoured by the situation she had filled, was held in universal reverence as the Inca's bride." (Prescott, *Peru*, Book I, chap. III.)

In reading Prescott's account of the kindling of the Sacred Fire in Peru, the parallel between ancient Rome and the religious worship of the Incas, becomes even more apparent.

The latter kindled their sacred fire by means of a concave mirror of polished metal, which, collecting the rays of the sun into a focus upon a quantity of dried cotton, speedily caused combustion. It was the expedient used on the like occasions in ancient Rome, at least under the reign of the pious Numa. When the sky was overcast, and the face of the good deity was hidden from his worshippers, which was esteemed a bad omen, fire was obtained by means of friction.

The sacred flame was entrusted to the care of the Virgins of the Sun ; and if, by any neglect, it was suffered to go out in the course of the year, the event was regarded as a calamity that boded some strange disaster to the monarchy.

HESTIA OF GREECE

IN Ancient Greece, as in the early days of Rome, and indeed in numerous other countries, the guarding of a perpetual fire became part of a religious cult.

Remembering the essential value of fire to primitive peoples, it is not surprising to find that the early mind shewed this tendency to attach enormous importance to the mystery and utility of fire, and as a corollary, to invest it with mystic powers, and to make it an object of worship.

In Greece, Hestia was the counterpart, to some extent, of Vesta in Rome.

Hestia, the daughter of Chronos and Rhea, was a " numen " rather than a " dea," a personification of the hearth itself, and she never can be said to have attained the status of a goddess in the same sense as Pallas Athene or Aphrodité.

As the Greek mind at an early date rose far above the animistic religious idea, Hestia could never be to them what Vesta was to the Romans.

Between Hestia and Agni the Hindu fire god of the Vedic religion the parallel is far closer, although Agni enjoyed a greater prestige than Hestia.

There was only one temple of Hestia in Greece (although unlike Vesta there were several statues), and the inference from this is that she was not generally recognised as a personal goddess.

As to the connection between Hestia and Vesta, the authorities differ somewhat.

According to Professor Rose in his *Handbook of Greek Mythology*, Hestia the fire deity is the same as Vesta, etymologically and otherwise.

Frazer, on the other hand (*Commentaries on the Fasti of Ovid*), says :

" Though the name Vesta was certainly not borrowed from the Greeks, we may acquiesce in the etymological identity of Vesta and Hestia, despite certain philological difficulties."

All authorities, however, are agreed that whilst the perpetual fire was guarded and had its priestesses in Ancient Greece, as in Rome, at no time nor place was the same importance attached to the Greek cult, nor did its priestesses enjoy the same distinction or place in the religious life of the community, as did the Vestal Virgins of Rome.

Frazer gives numerous instances of the perpetual fire being guarded in Greece, notably in the Prytaneum at Delphi, which particular fire was watched over not by virgin priestesses, but by widows.

Elsewhere he tells us that the sacred fire in Greece was guarded by women who had ceased to have sexual relations with men.

Herein lies the chief point of difference between the Greek and Roman cults, and this difference is so fundamental that it appears to discount any idea of the Roman cult being borrowed from Greece.

The central ideas, of course, are the same in each case, the sacredness of fire, the reverence for the hearth on which it was kindled, and the allegorical significance of the hearth itself as the centre of family life.

The altar of Hestia remained in the principal room of every Greek house, even when the blazing fire originally associated with her altar had been removed to the kitchen.

On the altar of Hestia sacrifices were offered to all the gods, and such altars were found not only in private houses, but also in the Prytaneia and town halls throughout Greece.

The first portion of what was eaten or drunk was sacrificed to Hestia, and at all births, marriages or deaths her altar was garlanded with flowers and sprinkled with incense.

Men swore by the hearth-altar of Hestia, much as a Viking swore by his sword-blade.

Farnell (*Cults of the Greek States*) writes :

" Hestia was originally not the goddess who made the hearth holy, but was in essence the hearth itself, and this religious perception belonged to the animistic or pre-animistic period.

The attempt to make her a personal goddess at a later date was a comparative failure."

PART II

TOPOGRAPHY OF ANCIENT BUILDINGS, STREETS, AND MONUMENTS CONNECTED WITH THE CULT

THE REGIA

ONE of the most interesting of the discoveries which have been made in Rome was the excavation, a few years ago, of the remains of the Regia, in the earlier days probably the residence of the Rex Sacrorum, but in classical times the official residence of the Pontifex Maximus, the Chapter House, so to speak, of the Roman religion.

This was partly uncovered in 1882 and covered up again after a brief period. At the time it was considered to be part of the original Atrium Vestæ, but in 1886 it was demonstrated that the remains then visible were those of the Regia, and this hypothesis is undoubtedly correct.

Servius (*ad Æneid*, VIII., 363) places the locality exactly. He says :

" Who does not know that the Regia, where Numa lived, was at the foot of the Palatine and inside the ground of the Forum Romanum ? "

Although this may not point out the actual spot where Numa dwelt, it is quite admissible evidence as to the position of the Regia, a building well known in historical times.

The Atrium Regium was the official residence of the king as High Priest, and after the abolition of the monarchy it became the residence of the republican High Priest.

This statement is borne out by the following extracts from Latin writers :

" Numa at first resided on the Quirinal Hill, then in the Regia, as it is still called, near the Temple of Vesta." (Solinus, A.D. Third Century, I, 21 : p. 6, Mommsen's Edition. 1895.)

" Numa erected a royal palace called the Regia, near

the Temple of Vesta, where he passed most of his time."
(Plutarch, *Numa*, 14.) "There they (the Romans)
engaged again, and repulsed the Sabines as far as the
Palace, now called the Regia, and the Temple of
Vesta." (Plutarch, *Romulus*, 18 sub. fin.)

Ovid (*Tristia*, III, 1, 30) speaks of it as a small
edifice : "This was the little palace of the ancient
Numa "—and in *Fasti*, VI, 263 : "This little spot
which now supports the Atrium Vestæ, was in those
days the mighty palace of unshorn Numa."

This little palace which became the Regia has been
discovered occupying the space between the Temple
of Vesta and the Sacra Via in front of the Temple of
Antoninus Pius and Faustina : having its north side
of 63 ft. parallel with the Sacred Way. Its west side,
towards the Forum, is 79 ft. 10 in. The south side,
separated from the Temple of Vesta by a vicus, or
municipal boundary, is 83 ft. long ; 20 ft. of this, at
the south-west corner, seems to have been an addition.
The east side, which was the front, is 39 ft. long. Thus
it is shaped like a key-stone, an apt symbol, for religion
is the key-stone of the State.

On its west, or Forum side was an open court,
(atrium), afterwards occupied by the Temple-Tomb of
Cæsar, whose body was cremated in the Forum.

"Where is the former Regia of the Romans."
(Appian, *Bell. Civ.*, II, 148.)

The Regia, and with it some of the adjacent temples,
was several times burned down, with consequent
changes in the manner of its erection. In 241 B.C., the
Temple of Vesta being on fire, Cæcilius Metellus, the
Pontifex Maximus, saved the sacred objects from the
flames. (Livy, *Epit.*, XIX.)

" Metellus lost his sight whilst snatching the Palladium from the Temple of Vesta." (Pliny, *N.H.*, VII,
141.) "He saved the Palladium." (Valerius Max.,
I, 4, 5.) "The man who saved the trembling Minerva
from the blazing fane." (Juvenal, *Sat.*, III, 138 *seq.*
See also Dionysius II, 66 ; Cicero, *pro Scauro*, 47 ;
Ovid, *Fasti*, VI, 437 *sqq.*) This last passage is referred

to again in the section dealing with the shrine of Ops Consiva.

In 210 B.C. a fire broke out at the Septem Tabernæ and the Atrium Regium was involved. (Livy, XXVI, 27.)

The Temple of Vesta was with difficulty preserved, chiefly by the exertions of thirteen slaves, who were manumitted at the public cost. (*Ib.*)

Investigation disclosed a formidable conspiracy among noble Campanian youths, who had deliberately caused the fire. Q. Flaccus the ex-consul, stated that certain Campanians had deserted to Hannibal and that others had come to Rome with the intention of firing the city, aiming specially at the Temple of Vesta, the sacred fire and the relics.

" Their aim had been the Temple of Vesta and the eternal fires and the fateful pledge of Roman power, hidden in the sanctuary."

" Vestæ ædem petitam et æternos ignes et conditum in penetrali fatale pignus imperii Romani." (Livy, XXVI, 27, 14.)

The guilty persons were punished with exemplary severity and the Regia rebuilt in the following year. Julius Obsequens, a fourth century recorder of ancient prodigies informs us that in A.U.C. 606 (148 B.C.) " a fire ravaged Rome, when the Regia also was consumed; the Sacrarium (of Ops Consiva) and one of the two bay-trees were saved uninjured out of the midst of the flames." Hence the two bay trees now planted there. (Obsequens, 19, p. 156, Rossbach.)

To this period we may attribute the opus incertum construction found within the Tufa walls.

The Regia was again destroyed in the fire of Nero (Tacitus, *Annals*, XV, 41) in A.D. 64.

A shield is said to have fallen from Heaven in the days of Numa, and the King afraid of its being stolen had others made like it. (Dionysius, II, 71 ; Ovid, *F.*, III, 373.) It was called Ancile, from its shape, like the figure eight. The Ancilia were carried in procession by the Salii on the first of March.

There were kept in the Regia the Spears of Mars, in

a Sacrarium, and it was looked upon as a bad omen if
they shook, as is said to have happened at the time of
Cæsar's murder. (Dion Cassius, XLIV, 17.) Aulus
Gellius also (IV, 6, 2) speaks of the spears moving.

Within the precincts of the Regia was a shrine to
Ops Consiva, goddess of the seed-time, to which
allusion will be made later, but we know little of the
ritual of her worship except that when he entered her
chapel, the Pontifex Maximus wore the suffibulum of
the Vestals and the præfericulum (a special vessel)
was used. (Varro, *L.L.*, VI, 21, and Festus, 249.)

In these buildings were deposited the general
records of the city, and also the register of magistrates,
and it was to these records later that the chroniclers of
Rome's history had recourse. Outside the Regia in
earlier times was the "tabula dealbata," a whited
panel whereon were inscribed the most important
incidents of the year. When the walls of the Regia
were reconstructed in the course of some eighteen
years (from 54 to 36 B.C.), pilasters of marble were
used for the inscription of the Fasti, as the records
were termed ; these, fortunately, proved more lasting
than the parchment of earlier times. For much of this,
Domitius Calvinus must be held in high remembrance,
for it was he who, after the Regia was gutted by fire in
36 B.C., rebuilt its walls in this way, and caused the inscriptions to be engraved. (Dion Cassius, XLVIII, 42.)

He was consul in 40 B.C. An altar at the Temple
of Jupiter Victor was erected by him out of the spoils
of war. This was the Domitius Calvinus who commanded Cæsar's centre at Pharsalia and retrieved the
day when the wings were defeated.

The wall of *opus reticulatum* and piers of travertine ;
the chamber with the mosaic pavement at the south-
west corner, and the travertine wall inside the late
steps on the north side appear to be of this date. It
was destroyed in Nero's fire with the delubra Vestæ and
the Penates (Tacitus, *Ann.*, XV, 41) and restored by
Vespasian. The brick remains are of this date.

It is to this period that the blocks of white Luneuse

(Carrara) marble belong ; they have marginal draft edges, but some of the drafted lines are cut irrespective of the joints, to give the walls a uniform appearance, as in the marble walls of the round Temple of Hercules, which, as it now stands, is also of this date.

The construction also agrees. Carrara marble[1] was not used in Rome before the time of Nero.

In the reign of Commodus in A.D. 191 a terrible fire broke out in Rome. It was an extremely dry year and there was a general impression of impending calamity. The stars were visible at midday and there were many portents.

Either by accident or, as it was supposed, from the emission of fire from the earth, the Temple of Peace caught fire. The fire spread into a great conflagration, which involved also the Temple of Vesta.

The Vestal Virgins were taken by surprise, and in their hurry and confusion neglected to cover the Palladium, which they snatched from the flames and took by the Sacred Way to the imperial palace. Thus for the first time the figure was exposed to the view of man. This is Herodian's account (I, 14, 4) :

" And then also as the Temple of Vesta had been consumed by fire, the image of Pallas was seen exposed, an image which the Romans reverence and conceal, after it had been brought from Troy, as report has it. And then for the first time since its arrival from Troy to Italy the men of our days beheld it.

For the maiden priestesses of Vesta, having seized the image, carried it with them through the midst of the Sacred Way to the Palace of the Emperor."

When Cæcilius Metellus (see p. 100) risked his life to save the thrice-sacred Palladium from Vesta's sanctuary, and although successful, lost his eyesight in the heroic effort, he was rewarded by the honours of a statue with an epigraph erected on the Capitol, the unique privilege of going to the Senate House

[1] Pliny (*N.H.*, XXXVI, 14) after speaking of Parian marble, says that many whiter marbles had subsequently been discovered and also recently (nuper) in the quarries of Luna.

in a chariot, instead of on foot, and the agnomen of " PIUS " which was made transmissible to his descendants.

The Temple partly escaped, or was restored after, the fire of A.D. 191, for the word REGIA occurs on a piece of the marble plan of Septimius Severus and it is represented in the background of the relief (in the Uffizi gallery) of the Temple of Vesta, which shows the south side, having at each end a fluted composite pilaster.

A piece of moulded base exists at the north corner, and part of a fluted pilaster on the travertine pier on the west side ; one of the capitals was built into the shrine of Mercury at the entry to the Atrium Vestæ, when that was injudiciously restored in 1898, and two pieces of the entablature are opposite the east corner.

The original construction of Numa—square blocks of tufa stone—exists on all four sides.

The Regia apparently suffered in the great fire under Maximinus in A.D. 238 (Herodian, VII, 12) when its area was covered with ashes and debris. Over this a later edifice was erected, of which remains exist, built of the old material, along the east front over the area of the Regia.

The main entry into the edifice was from the Via Sacra, a frontage of 63 feet, approached by a flight of steps still existing, forming an angle with the original north tufa wall of the Regia.

At each end is a base of red granite ; the north one supporting a column of cipoline marble. Behind this column is a well lined with tufa, a piece of *opus incertum* supporting some travertine, and marble of the " late edifice." Thus, all through, the construction and the historical notices agree. In the Vicus near the southeast angle of the Regia is a well with a good spring of water. This spring was probably reserved for the special use daily of the Vestal Virgins.

The following references will indicate how this group of buildings formed part of the official and social life in Rome.

Cicero (*ad Atticum*, X, 3b) says :

" On the same day, the seventh before the Ides, I dictate this letter to you and on the day before the Ides I had written a longer one in my own hand. They say you were seen in the Regia and I don't blame you, seeing that I myself have not escaped the same censure."[1]

Atticus had gone there to meet Cæsar, for the letter proceeds to discuss the actions and sayings of the latter.

As Pontifex Maximus, Cæsar transacted business there, although he did not live there, but " in Sacra Via domo publica," that is to say in the Sacra Via in a public residence. But in his speech the same year (pro rege Deiotaro, Sec. 2), Cicero says he is speaking within the walls of a private residence (intra domesticos parietes). Did this later become Cæsar's official dwelling ?

In this connection it is worth while to trace the residences of Cæsar.

" He lived first in the Subura in a modest house ; but after his High Priesthood on the Sacred Way in a house belonging to the State."[2]

This change is explained by the fact that in 45 B.C., by a decree of the Senate, a house, belonging to the State, was granted to Cæsar as a residence. (Dion Cassius, XLIII, 44.) Was this the *freehold* of the private house, or did he convert part of the latter into a State dwelling ?

This house, which was distinct from the Regia, is shown by the previous quotation to have been in the Sacred Way.[3]

[1] " A.D. VII Idus alteram tibi eodem die hanc epistulam dictavi et pridie dederam mea manu longiorem. Visum te aiunt in regia nec reprehendo, quippe cum ipse istam reprehensionem non fugerim."

[2] " Habitavit primo in Subura modicis ædibus; post autem pontificatum maximum (63 B.C.) in sacra via domo publica." (Suet., *Cæsar*, XLVI.)

[3] Warde Fowler says that in historical times a white victim was taken to the Capitol by way of the Via Sacra in procession, and the term Via Sacra, according to Festus was probably derived from this procession.

Horace possibly had this in mind when he wrote " Dum Capitolium scandet cum tacita virgine pontifex."

The official residence of the Rex Sacrorum was actually at the east end of the Sacra Via near the Arch of Titus (Wissowa).

If he had actually lived in the Regia, Cicero would not have called it a private residence, nor Suetonius a residence belonging to the public.

If they had meant the Regia, they would have said the Regia, as all other authors do.

Cicero says " private residence " ; this shows that it could not have been the Regia, for it is a well-known fact that the Regia was open to the public.

The public gift of the house on the Sacra Via appears to have been made when Cæsar was perpetual dictator. Cicero, by the way, remarked that he was himself nearly murdered close to the Regia. (*Pro Milone*, 14.)

When on March 6th, 12 B.C., Augustus was elected Pontifex Maximus, he refused to use the Regia for his official residence in that capacity, but instead he gave it over into the charge of the Vestals, because it had a common wall with their premises. (Dion Cassius, LIV, 27.) This is confirmed by Ovid (*Fasti*, VI, 263) and by Servius (*in Æneid*, VII, 153), where he writes, " Now this had been the Regia of Numa Pompilius, but it (i.e. the Senate) used to meet in the Atrium Vestæ which was some distance from their temple."

Augustus, furthermore, when in 12 B.C. he became Pontifex Maximus and lived on the Palatine, did not accept a grant of any State buildings, but actually made over to the State part of his own house, because the Pontifex Maximus had to live entirely on state premises. (Dion Cassius, LIV, 27.)

Two statues out of the four which had supported the tent of Alexander the Great were consecrated before the Regia by Augustus. (Pliny, *N.H.*, XXXIV, 48.)

These are probably the statues shown on each side of the Temple of Vesta on a coin of Vespasian. The old palace of Numa, although given into the charge of the Vestals by Augustus was, in the second and third centuries, still called the Regia and used for the transaction of religious affairs. (Pliny the Younger, *Ep.*, IV, 116; Plutarch, *Rom. Quæst.*, 97; Solinus, I, 21, p. 6, Mommsen's Ed., 1895.)

THE LATE EDIFICE

TREBELLIUS POLLIO, writing in the fourth century, says :

"In short, there was up to this time (A.D. 268) a statue at the foot of the Mount of Romulus (the Palatine), that is, at the entrance to the Sacred Way, between the Temples of Faustina and Vesta near the Arch of the Fabii, upon which statue was inscribed 'to Gallienus the Younger' (Gallieno Minori) with the word Saloninus added, so that the meaning of his name might be clear."[1] Asconius (*in Verr.*, Act. I, 7, 19) says, "The Fornix Fabius is close to the Regia on the Sacred Way."

The piers of this arch still exist on the south side of the temple-tomb of Cæsar, and behind them, to the east, the remains of the Regia have been now discovered bordering on the Sacred Way.

Now if the statue of Gallienus the Younger stood in the angle between the arch and temples of Vesta and Faustina, it must have stood somewhere within the precincts of the Regia ; and as Pollio does not mention the Regia, we must conclude that it did not exist in his day, but was perhaps destroyed in the great fire in A.D. 238 (Herodian, VII, 12, Capitolinus, *Max. et Balb.*, 9) ; and when the property of the Vestals fell into the hands of the Church in 383 under Gratian, the very late edifice, the remains of which we have pointed out, was erected on its site and out of the ancient material.

Part of an inscription exists built into the north wall

---

[1] " Quæ haberet inscriptum Gallieno Minori Salonino additum ex quo eius nomen intelligi poterit." (*Gallieni duo*, XIX, 4.)

of the chamber on the right-hand side of the eastern entry to the late edifice :

P

ELIO

CAESAR

ANI

N

L. Aelius Cæsar was consul with P. Cœlius Balbinus, A.D. 137. He had been adopted by Hadrian in 136, and died on 1st January, 138.

It would appear, however, to be different in character from the Fasti series, and does not belong to them.

THE FASTI

IT has been considered that the Fasti Triumphales et Consulares were engraved on the exterior walls of the Regia, but this is at least doubtful, for many of the existing fragments date from the time of Augustus, i.e. prior to the most destructive fires, which marble could have withstood with difficulty.

The accounts all connect the finding of these inscriptions with the Temple of Castor and Pollux, on the east and south sides, in 1547 and 1816. Other fragments were found in 1872 and 1879 by the temple of the deified Cæsar ; also in 1898.

Panvinio, who was present at the discovery in 1547, says :

" The first fragments were found at a ruined edifice which has *the form of an hemicycle*."

The only ruin in the Forum that has this form is the Temple of Cæsar with the Rostra Julia in front of it, which is hemicycle.

The lofty platform of the temple of the deified Cæsar would be a most appropriate place for these records. Of these I saw the first one, found in 1872 in front of the Rostra Julia, where it remained for some years, and then was removed to the Conservatori Palace. It reads :

ROMVLVS. MARTIS. F.REX.
ANN DE CAENINENSIBVS.
K. MAR

MARTIS. F. REX. II.

Romulus, Son of Mars King in the (number missing) year of the City. From the spoils of Cænina March 1st [Romulus] son of Mars, King. For the second time [remainder missing].

This agrees with Livy (I, 10), other fragments being found at the same time.

Ligorio, who was also present at the discovery in 1547, speaks of a building upon which were the Fasti being destroyed for material for St. Peter's; that many portions of it were broken up, and that then Cardinal Alexander Farnese stepped in and saved them; Michael Angelo building them into the wall of the Conservatori Palace of the Capitol in such a manner as to represent the edifice from which they were taken.

Ligorio says it took thirty days to destroy the building.

This would be quite possible if the blocks had to be stripped off the podium of Cæsar's temple, but certainly not if taken off the solid marble walls of the Regia, which in fact was, as has been demonstrated, then no longer existing, having been destroyed (apparently in the fire of 238) to a considerable extent.

Ligorio gives a drawing of the building he saw destroyed, which, decidedly fanciful, in no way corresponds with the remains of the Regia now discovered. He calls it a *vero jano summo quatrifronte*, confusing it with the upper Janus of Horace (*Epist.*, I, 54), which has reference to a part of the Forum and not to a building.

He depicts two somewhat deep rectangular niches heavily decorated with Tuscan columns on each side supporting a pediment, at the apex of which is an eagle. Behind, but attached to them, he says, there was a façade surmounted by a pediment with a very florid cornice. Between the niches there was an open archway, within which was to be seen a clustered column, with open arches springing to the right and left.

This does not agree in any way with the reliefs and coins showing the Temple of Cæsar, but curiously enough it does somewhat with the Arch of Augustus erected adjoining the temple to commemorate the battle of Actium.

Dion Cassius (LI, 19) agrees as to its site, as

depicted on a coin of the Vinician family, inasmuch as the arch is triple, the centre one being arched and the side ones horizontal, with columns supporting a pediment. (See Donaldson's *Architectura Numismatica*, p. 228.)

The façade erected by Michael Angelo is 24 ft. long, and composed of blocks of Greek marble. They have not drafted edges. This does not agree with the blocks of Carrara marble found on the Regia site, which have marginal draft edges.

This façade of 24 ft. would not fit any of the sides of the Regia, and it does not represent the Regia as now known to us.

When the Forum occasionally was under water, on-lookers might well realise once more the flood described by Horace in 12 B.C. (Dion Cassius, LVI, 27.)

" We have seen the waves of the tawny Tiber, violently hurled back from the Etruscan bank, rush on to fling down the monuments of the King and Vesta's fanes (*Odes*, I, 2, 13).

SACRARIA (CHAPELS)

AS has been stated, the Regia, the official residence and office of the Pontifex Maximus, was the religious centre of Ancient Rome. Furthermore the principal State documents, both civil and religious, were kept there, the State Calendars, the Budget of Yearly Events (Annales) the Religious Laws (relating to marriage, wills, death duties, etc.), the Decrees and Commentaries, the Lists of the members of the Sacred College, past and present, the Official Transactions (Acta) of the College, and all the Formulas dealing with the forms of prayer, dedications, vows and sacrifices.

SACRARIUM OF OPS CONSIVA

WITHIN the west angle of the original edifice of the Regia is an enclosure 34 feet long and 17 feet wide ; inside this is a rectangular tufa platform 23 feet long and 23½ wide, in the centre of which is a course of brown tufa stone 8 inches high (the course of red brick on the top of this is modern) and 15 inches in diameter.

I would suggest as worthy of consideration that the Penus Vestae possibly was in the shrine of the Goddess Ops Consiva ; if so, it was here that the Palladium, the image of Minerva, which was said to have fallen from heaven to Troy, was placed. What the Palladium really was, is something of a mystery. The ordinary educated Roman would naturally think of the Palladium of the second book of the *Æneid*, an armed statue of Minerva. Here are two accounts from Apollodorus and Procopius respectively.

Apollodorus (III, 12, 3) says :

" Ilius beheld the Palladium lying in front of the tent and it was two cubits high standing with the feet together, holding in the right hand an uplifted spear, and in the other a distaff and spindle." This measurement would make it about three feet high in English dimensions.

Procopius (A.D. 550) says :

" Where the Palladium is now the Romans do not know, but shew a figure of it graven in stone, standing in my time in the Temple of Fortune, before the bronze statue of Minerva fighting, her lance in rest ; yet in a long robe, and with a face not like her Grecian statues, but as the Egyptians made them. They of

Constantinople say that Constantine buried the statue in the Forum bearing his name." (*De Bell. Goth.*, I, 13).

This and the Ancilia or sacred shields of the Salii, which latter were kept in the Sacrarium Martis, were the most revered relics of Rome.

" Numa gave to the Vestal Virgins for custody the Ancilia and Palladium, in a sense secret pledges of empire " (Secreta quædam imperii pignora)—" and above all the hearth of Vesta." (Florus, I, 2.)

" The famous Palladium, which, they say, is kept by the Holy Virgins." (Dionysius, I, 69.) " The memorable pledge of empire in the hidden shrine, Pallas by no male beheld." (Lucan, IX, 993.)

" The filleted priestess leads the Vestal choir, to whom it is permitted to see the Trojan Minerva." (Lucan, I, 598.) Hence the extreme sanctity of this shrine of Ops Consiva.

" The Sacrarium which is in the Regia, into which no one but the High Priest and the High Vestal can enter."[1] (Varro, *L.L.*, VI, 21.)

But Lucan (I, 598, and IX, 994) ; Plutarch (in *Camillus*) and Ovid (*Fasti*, VI, 254 and 450) say that no men could enter.

This seems most probable, as these sacred relics were under their special protection.

Ovid tells us that before Metellus went in when the buildings were on fire in 241 B.C., he implored the gods to pardon him if he entered the shrine, though a man. (*Fasti*, VI, 449, 450.)

But if he had, as High Priest, the right of entry, there was no occasion for him to ask forgiveness before entering to save the Palladium, which was kept there. (See Plutarch in *Camillus*, Lucan, IX, 994.)

Pliny, however, who mentions the relics in connection with Metellus (VII, 141), Valerius Maximus (I, 4, 5), Livy (V, 52, and Epit. 19), and Dionysius (II, 66), all speak of the Palladium as kept in the Temple of Vesta.

[1] Ut eo præter Virgines Vestales et sacerdotem publicum introeat nemo.

Possibly, however, they are to be considered as using the term for the whole group of the Vestal edifices.

Ops, the wife of Saturn, was worshipped under different names. In sculpture she is represented as a matron holding a loaf in her left hand. The people paid homage to her in a sitting position.

" Therefore she is called Consiva, and is esteemed to be the Earth ; and therefore she is worshipped by the Roman people in the Regia, because the earth gives all wealth (opes) to the human race." (Festus, s.v. *Opima Spolia*, p. 186.)

Festus also tells us that " the bronze dish, without handles, called *Præfericulum*, used in the sacrifices, was kept in the shrine of Ops Consiva." (249 Mueller.) And he identifies her with the Bona Dea, when he says, " The sacrificial knife, *Secespita*, used by the higher grades of priests (i.e. the flamen, flaminicæ, virgines, pontifices), was kept in the shrine of the Bona Dea."[1] Both of these instruments are represented on the frieze of the Temple of Vespasian in the Forum and on the Arch of the Silversmiths in the Velabrum.

Ops as the Bona Dea, the Goddess of Chastity, was specially venerated by the Vestals ; in fact, the Vestal Claudia Quinta erected a temple to her on the Aventine (Ovid, *Fasti*, V, 155). The altar, in the gallery of the Capitol, has perhaps some connection with this temple.[2]

It was on the night of December 3rd, 62 B.C., when the secret rites of the Bona Dea were being observed in the house of Cæsar, as Prætor, which adjoined the Regia to the east, that Clodius entered dressed as a woman, and " wandering about the great house " (Plutarch, *Cæsar*, 10) was discovered.

In 44 B.C., the year of Cæsar's murder, the folding

[1] This restoration of the text by Orsini and the identification of Ops with Bona Dea are now, however, rejected by many modern scholars.

[2] Cornelius Labeo (*Macrobius*, I, 12, 21–22) identifies Ops and the Bona Dea.

doors of the shrine of Ops were fractured, and the trees and very many houses were entirely overthrown. (Julius Obsequens at p. 68, 128.)

In the Gallery of the Capitol is an altar to Minerva (No. 47) found in the Velabrum, on which is a relief of Numa consigning the Palladium to the Vestals.

Plutarch (*in Camillus*) ; Ovid (*Fasti*, VI, 254 and 421, *sq.*) ; and Horace (*Ep.*, II, 2, 114), all allude to the secret shrine and objects.

When the Gauls were advancing on Rome, the sacred objects were buried in earthen jars (doliolis) in a chapel adjoining the residence of the Flamen Quirinalis, where later it was considered profane to spit. (Livy, V, 40.)

Varro (*L.L.*, V, 157) confirms this and says it was near the Cloaca Maxima. Plutarch (*in Camillus*, XX, *sub fin.*) says it was buried underground in the Temple of Quirinus, and that the place from those jars was still called Doliola. This temple was on the Quirinal Hill.

There are many references to a Temple of Ops in Cicero's *Philippics* (I, 17, II, 35, 93, etc.). All of these relate to its use as a storehouse of specie and not for religious ends. This probably was her other shrine on the Capitol.

Professor A. Clark remarks in a note : " The remains of the Temple of Ops are still visible near the Forum adjoining the Temple of Saturn."

Reference has already been made to the rescue of the Palladium by Cæcilius Metellus from the burning temple, and to the exposure of the Palladium by the Vestals in saving it from its shrine in the fire of A.D. 192.

The violence done to the Palladium by Heliogabalus is referred to in Part I (pp. 72, 74).

THE HOLY OF HOLIES

(PENUS OR PENETRALIA)

THE word Penus means, "that which is inside the house" (cf. *penetralia*, *penitus*), it also means a store or sanctuary.

It must be remembered that every Roman house had its own Storeroom (penus), which was deemed holy because the Penates, or Gods of the Storeroom, dwelt therein.

Thus in every house Vesta, the Goddess of the Hearth, was intimately bound up in the Roman mind with the Penates, and was indeed reckoned as one of them.

It follows therefore that the Penus, already sacred in the common Roman home, became the Holy of Holies in the House of the Vestals.

Festus writes (250) :

" Penus vocatur locus intimus in æde Vestæ tegetibus sæptus, qui certis diebus circa Vestalia aperitur i dies religiosi habentur."

" Penus is the name of the inmost place in the temple of Vesta curtained by means of mats. It is opened on appointed days during the Festival of Vesta. Such days are of ill omen."

In the court on the north side of the shrine of Ops Consiva a sunken circular chamber was found, 10 ft. in diameter at its base, $14\frac{1}{2}$ ft. deep, domed in with concentric overlapping rings of tufa, like the treasure chamber of the Temple of Victory on the Palatine.

It is coated with a peculiar blue volcanic clay covered with white stucco. On a piece of the travertine coping-stone which closed it is cut the word " REGIA ".

This was, no doubt, the sacred store-chamber where the grain was stored, with which the Vestals made the *mola salsa* cake from May 7th to 14th. (Servius, on *Ecl.*, VIII, 82.)

These were also sometimes called " Februa." (Ovid, *Fasti*, II, 24.)

Within this chamber was found a wooden writing tablet (on which probably the tally was recorded), eighty finely worked bone *stili* or pens, some broken vases and bones. It was cleared out once a year, on June 15th, and the sweepings conveyed to a lane about the middle of the Clivus Capitolinus (the pathway from the Via Sacra to the top of the Capitol). It is shut off by the Porta Stercoraria. (Festus, 344. See also Varro, *L.L.*, VI, 32.) When the "Late Edifice" was erected, this chamber was converted into a rain cistern, and is now half full of water.

The sunken chamber just described was possibly the original Penus.

It appears that the Penetralia in the new home of the Vestals took the place of the Penus or sunken chamber in the original Regia. This was probably the chamber with the apse at the west end. Under the mosaic floor were found jars, forming a kind of sink.

The Penus was cleansed on June 15th of each year for the reception of the first fruits of the harvest, and was then closed until June 7th of the following year.

SACRARIUM MARTIS

TO the west of the Penus is a well of spring water, 16 ft. 8 in. deep, lined with blocks of tufa. To the north of the well is a small rectangular tufa base, 4 ft. by 4 ft. 10 in., upon which is cut a circle 2ft. 10 in. in diameter. Upon a loose stone is a part of an inscription.

It is probable that the marble altar, now on the steps of the Temple of Jupiter Victor on the Palatine, may have stood here. It is 3 ft. 1½ in. in diameter upon a travertine base of 3 ft. 5 in. by 3 ft. 4 in., and would fit.

It apparently belonged either to the Temple of Vesta or to the Regia, but it is inscribed :

CN. DOMITIVS. M.F. CALVINVS
PONTIFEX
COS. ITER. IMPER.
DE MANIBEIS

This agrees with the fact that Calvinus restored the Regia with spoil of the Spanish War. He was Consul for the second time in 40 B.C.

If so, is this not the altar of Mars which stood within the Sacrarium, where the Spears of Mars were kept, which rattled just before Cæsar's murder ?[1] (Dion Cassius, XLIV, 17.)

They served as an instrument to record earthquakes. Aulus Gellius (IV, 6, 1) records that in the Regia the Hastæ Martiæ moved. He preserves as to this the Senatus Consultum made on this occasion. Julius Obsequens records that the Spears in the Regia (the Hastæ Martiæ) moved more particularly in the years

[1] See, however, p. 133 *seq*. for a stronger hypothesis.

181, 117, 102, 98 and 95 B.C. Seismic disturbances were thus recorded.

Here were kept the Ancilia, or sacred shields of Mars. Only one was genuine and was said to have fallen from heaven in the reign of Numa, and the King, afraid of its being stolen, had others made like it. (Dionysius, II, 71 ; Ovid, *Fasti*, III, 381.) As already recorded, a similar story is told of the jars in one of which the Palladium was kept.

This shield was called " Ancile " from its shape like the figure 8.

The Ancilia were carried in procession by the Salii, or dancing priests of Mars, on March 1st.

At the race held in October (Equirria) the off horse of the winning chariot was sacrificed to Mars in the Campus Martius, and a contest then took place for the animal's head, between the inhabitants of the district of Subura (Suburanenses) and those of the Sacred Way (Sacravienses).

If the people of Subura obtained it, they placed it on the Turris Mamilia ; if the habitants of the Via Sacra were victorious, they placed it on the Regia. The tail was cut off, and the blood was distilled in the fire ; and with great quickness taken to the Regia. (Festus, p. 178.) It was there preserved and used as a fumigation on the festival of Pales, April 21st. (Ovid, *Fasti*, IV, 733.)

This curious custom has not escaped Plutarch in his *Romane Questions*.

" What is the cause," he asks, " that upon the thirteenth day of December, which in Latine they call the Ides of December, there is exhibited a game of chariots running for the prize, and the horse drawing on the right hand that winneth the victorie is sacrificed and consecrated unto Mars, and at the time thereof, there comes one behinde, that cutteth off his taile, which he carrieth immediately into the temple called Regia and therewith imbrueth the altar with blood, and for the head of the said horse, one troupe there is comming out of the street called Via Sacra, and another from that which they name Suburra, who encounter and trie out by fight who shall have it ? " (Plutarch, *Romane Questions*, Sec. 97. Translated by Philemon Holland.)

THE OFFICE OF THE KALATOR

AT the south-west corner of the Regia is a wedge-shaped chamber, below the level of the shrine of Ops Consiva, with remains of a black and white mosaic pavement, the threshold of which is formed with a piece of marble, with the following inscription, placed upside down :

KALATORES PONTIFICVM ET FLAMINIVM

Suetonius (*Gram.*, 12), speaks of the Kalator as an attendant on the priest.

In 1788 a list of names was found about this site presumably of other attendants and servers.

This was probably the waiting room of those attending on the Pontifex Maximus. It is outside the original tufa wall, and was evidently an addition of Domitius Calvinus. There is another small chamber on its north side with walls of *opus incertum* and *opus reticulatum*. The Kalator is spoken of in an inscription of Severus found in front of the Senate House.

THE SHRINE OF MERCURY

THIS is one of the Lares Compitales shrines, and stands on the right of the steps leading up into the Atrium Vestæ. It is represented on a bronze sestertius of Marcus Aurelius. Four Hermes busts support a circular pediment, in the Tympanum of which are represented the Tortoise from the shell of which Mercury made the lyre given to Apollo ; the Cock, his emblem of watchfulness ; the Ram, which he told the people of Tanagra to carry round their city in order to stop a plague ; the winged Cap, given to him by Jupiter ; the Caduceus, or wand of peace, given to him by Apollo ; and the magic purse.

On the obverse of this coin is the head of Marcus Aurelius, with the legend :

M. ANTONINVS. AVG. TR. P. XXVII

This coin as the inscription indicates was struck in the year A.D. 173. If, as I think, this represents the shrine, it must have been damaged in the fire and restored on other lines, judging from the fragments found in 1880.

The base of the statue of this shrine was fortunately found telling us the name :

DEO
MERCVRIO

On the bottom of the base is another inscription giving us the date of its re-erection, April 25th, A.D. 275 :

DEDICAT.
D. N. AVRELIANO. AVG. III. ET
MARCELLINO COSS.
VII. KAL. MAI.[1]

[1] Dedicated, the consuls being our Lord Aurelianus Augustus, for the third time, and Marcellinus, on the 25th April.

The brick podium of the shrine was cased with marble, one piece 1 ft. 4 in. high being in situ on the side towards the steps ; and it supported an entablature of Carrara marble formed by two half columns at the rear and two columns in front, of the fluted composite order; on the frieze is the inscription recording its erection by the Roman Senate and People.

SENATVS . POPVLVSQVE . ROMANVS
PECVNIA . PVBLICA . FACIENDAM . CVRAVIT[1]

in beautifully cut letters 5 in. high.

The podium is 4 ft. 7 in. high, 9 ft. 9 in. wide, 8 ft. 2 in. deep.

The fragments found were built up in November, 1898, with questionable taste. The plain travertine column does not belong to it, and the brick pier is altogether out of place. It should have had fluted columns if the capitals used belonged to it, which is very doubtful, as is shown in the left rear capital and fragment of a pilaster, and a sketch of Canina's from a relief. (Canina's sketches, however, are not to be relied upon entirely.)

From the relief in the Uffizi the capitals used belonged to the ruin on the north side of the Temple of Vesta, that is, the Regia.

---

[1] The Roman Senate and people had this erected at the public expense.

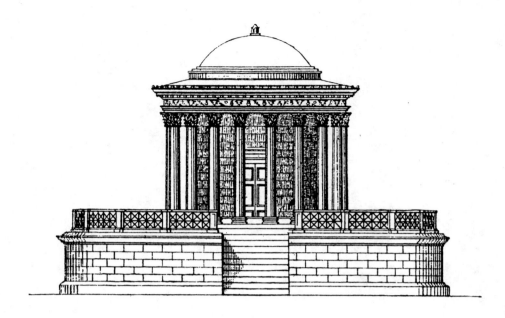

THE TEMPLE OF VESTA, RESTORED
(By permission of Dr. Forbes.)

THE TEMPLE OF VESTA

THE so-called " Temple of Vesta " in historical times stood at the northern foot of the Palatine Hill in the Forum.

Its situation on the flat ground suggests that it was a representation of the King's House of earlier times.

According to Varro (Aulus Gellius, XIV, 7, 7) it was not a temple in the accepted sense of the word, but a little round building, merely a copy of the round hut of the early kings, with walls of osiers and a primitive thatched roof (*v.* below, Ovid, *Fasti*, VI, 261–65).

Dionysius tells us that the first Temple of Vesta dates from the days of Numa Pompilius.

He writes :

" Numa when he became King did not disturb the private hearths (hestiæ) of the curiæ, but he established one common public one for them all in the ground that lay between the Capitol and the Palatine. The hills had been fortified already by a single encircling wall and the forum was in the middle. There the shrine was built, and he enacted that virgins should take charge of the rites according to customs and traditions of the Latins." (Dionysius, II, 66.)

The Temple was modelled from the primitive wattle hut (tugurium, capanna, tugurio) of the shepherds, the easiest form to construct and symbolical of the earth. Such was the first Temple of Vesta erected on a circular stone platform by Numa ; and so it probably lasted till Rome was fired by the Gauls.

" What you now see roofed with bronze you would then have seen roofed with thatch and the walls were wattled with pliant osiers." (Ovid, *Fasti*, VI, 261.)

" Yet the shape of the temple is said to have been

formerly as it now remains and the reason for the shape is before you to verify.

> Vesta is the same as Earth ; the unsleeping fire is under both.
> Earth and the hearth declare their own positions.
> Earth is like a ball, resting on no support. . . ."
>
> <div align="right">(<i>Ib.</i>, 265.)</div>

"Similar is the form of the temple, no angle projects in it.

A domed roof shields it from the rain." (<i>Ib.</i>, 281.)

" The roof of the temple was of Syracusan bronze." (Pliny, XXXIV, 13.)

The Senate could only sit in a place formally consecrated by augury. Hence Vesta's temple was never so consecrated, so that the Senate might not meet where the virgins were, for it had been formerly the palace of Numa Pompilius, but the Senate did so at the Atrium Vestæ some distance from the Temple. (Servius, <i>Æneid</i>, VII, 153.)

It should be noted here that the Roman Senate could not hold a meeting except on holy ground, and for this reason the Temple of Vesta was never consecrated, so as to prevent the Senate meeting in the place where the Vestal Virgins were.

The oldest representation that we have of the temple is on a silver denarius of the Cassia gens, struck by L. Cassius Longinus, the Prætor, 113 B.C.[1]

It represents a circular temple, with a domed roof surmounted by a statue. An altar is shown in the centre of the temple ; it looks like a bronze brazier standing on four legs. The medium of the fire must have been charcoal, that being the only combustible they could keep alight.

" To Numa is ascribed the sacred establishment of the Vestal Virgins, and the whole service with respect to the perpetual fire, which they watch continually.

---

[1] His severity in condemning two more Vestals (in addition to Æmilia who was condemned by the pontiffs) was proverbial. (Asconius, <i>Pro Milone</i>, 40.)

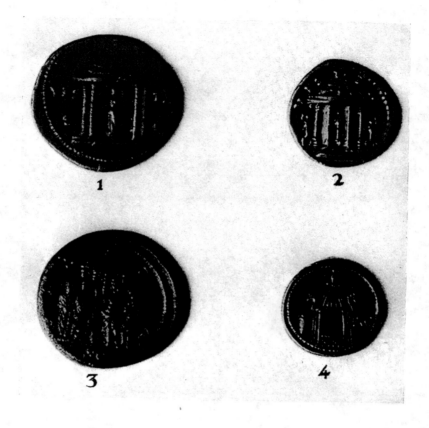

THE TEMPLE OF VESTA AS SHOWN ON COINS: (1) OF THE
CASSIA GENS, (2) VESPASIAN, (3) JULIA DOMNA, (4) DOMITIAN
This last shows the futile or water-jar of the vestals (p. 150).

. . . If it happens by accident to be put out, a new
fire is to be gained by drawing a pure and unpolluted
flame from the sunbeams. They kindle it with concave vessels of bronze, formed by the conic section of
a rectangled triangle, whose lines from the circumference meet in one central point. This being placed
against the Sun, causes its rays to converge in the
centre, which, by reflection, acquiring the force and
activity of fire, rarefy the air, and immediately kindle
such light and dry matter as they think fit to apply."
(Plutarch, in *Numa*, IX, Langhorne's trans.)

The fire was renewed annually on March 1st, New
Year's Day.

A similar ceremony of " rekindling the fire " is now
performed in the Portico of St. Peter's on the morning
of Easter Eve.

"A new fire is said to be made in the hidden shrine, and
the remade flame gains vitality." (Ovid, *Fasti*, III, 143.)

In 14 B.C. the Temple of Vesta was burnt, and the
sacred relics were removed by the Vestals to the house
of the Flamen Dialis on the Palatine, the High Vestal
being blind. (Dion Cassius, LIV, 24.) On May 19th,
64, it was destroyed in Nero's fire. (Tacitus, *A.*, 15,
41.) It was again consumed in the fire under Commodus in 191 (Herodian, I, 14, 4), and rebuilt by
the Empress Julia Pia Domna.[1]

A gold coin of Vespasian's represents the Temple,
approached by a flight of steps, having a statue on each
side of the temple, a circular altar within the temple,
a Vestal standing on the far side.

A denarius of the Empress Julia represents the re-
dedication of the temple after she had rebuilt it. In
front of the temple is a circular altar, with three Vestals
standing on either side, all six being veiled. One on
the right, is pouring out a libation ; one on the left,
is sprinkling salt (p. 153).

In the background is the temple, represented with
a lattice between the columns.

This is similarly shown on a bronze of Lucilla,

[1] Domna is late Latin for domina.

daughter of M. Aurelius, wife of L. Verus Piso, who (Piso) had been adopted by Galba.

Piso was killed at the doors of the temple of Vesta, after hiding in the chamber of one of the slaves. (Tacitus, *Hist.*, I, 43 ; Plutarch, *in Galba*, XXVII.)

THE TEMPLE OF VESTA
From an ancient relief in the Uffizi Gallery, Florence.
(By permission of Dr. Forbes.)

REPRESENTATIONS OF THE TEMPLE OF VESTA

A BEAUTIFUL relief of this last Temple of Vesta exists in the Uffizi Palace at Florence, over the door leading into the hall of the Faun. It shows the door with four columns on its right, facing towards the east, whilst it is approached by seven steps ; the columns are fluted with composite capitals, peculiarly short, the lower part below the Ionic volute being composed of aloe leaves.

One of the capitals can yet be seen temporarily placed over the inscription of the Shrine of Mercury. (This capital was used in restoring the shrine in November, 1898.) It can be compared with the relief which indicates its proper position.

Between the columns and over the doors, which open outwards, is a lattice of open-worked marble, agreeing with the coin of Julia Domna. I have been told that a piece of this screen is to be seen in the Stadium of the Palatine, taken there as building material with the pedestal to the High Vestal Cœlia Claudiana, but I have not been able to find it.

The object of this screen is obvious, indeed it was a necessity. The fire perpetually burning was composed of charcoal, and this screen allowed the fumes to escape and the fresh air to come in ; otherwise the Vestals watching the fire would be in danger of suffocation.

The pattern of the screen was something like that over the doors of the Pantheon.

To the left of the door is to be seen an old oak tree.

This is the celebrated " Capillata," or the tree upon which were hung the locks of the young girl which were cut off upon her initiation into the service of Vesta. (Pliny, *N.H.*, XVI, 235.)

In the background of the relief is shown a building which projects above and beyond the Temple on either side, showing that it was larger and loftier than the temple.

At each end is a fluted pilaster, or engaged column, which might more simply be described as an apparent column.

These columns support an entablature with plain mouldings forming the architrave, frieze and cornice which rise above the roof of the Temple.

This represents that part of the Vestals' convent as it was restored by Julia Domna Pia after the fire of 191 A.D.; its ruins may be seen to the left of the Temple, where some of the tufa *opus quadratum* of Numa can still be seen ; its front has been excavated some time.

The square composite capitals of the pilasters as shown on the relief agree in their peculiarity with those of the Temple of Vesta, and one of these can be examined, as it stands with the capital of the temple above described, supporting the inscription of the Shrine of Mercury near the entry to the Vestals' home.

The part below the Ionic is formed with the leaves of the aloe instead of the acanthus plant as usual.

Part of the fluted pilaster remains below the capital. It has been utilised in restoring the shrine of Mercury in 1898.

In the relief there is a peculiarity about the podium of the Temple.

It is lofty, the bases of the columns resting on pedestals which project from the circular platform, and the steps stand out well beyond their line. All this agrees with the actual ruins and remains.

The original tufa platform of Numa, still existing, was raised by Julia Domna ; making the Temple more commanding. Remains of the later marble casing lying about agree with the relief, and the remains of the stairs still project well beyond the rotundity of the platform.

The statue shown in the coin of Julia Domna as surmounting the dome is not represented on the relief, but the ornamental pedestal on which it stood is there.

The Temple was excavated in 1549 when it was

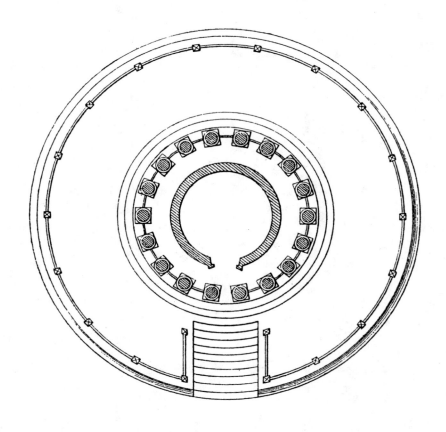

PLAN OF THE TEMPLE OF VESTA, DESTROYED IN 1549,
DISCOVERED IN 1877

(By permission of Dr. Forbes.)

found to be in an excellent state of preservation. It was then destroyed for the sake of the material. Panvinio made a plan of it (Vatican Codex, 3439, f. 28), which shows that it had eighteen columns.

In the Uffizi there is a design by Baldassarre Peruzzi, 1520, said to have been copied by him from a relief on the façade of the Lateran hospital, but it is no longer there.

It represents a circular temple approached by a flight of three steps, which run all round the podium, and shows the door and four columns to the right.

Over the door and between the first two columns is a screen of marble work differing in its detail from that of the relief mentioned above. Its roof is surmounted by an ornament similar to that shown in the coins of Vespasian.

Canina gives a sketch (V; II, plate 64), from the fragment of a relief, the whereabouts of which is unknown. The viewer is looking towards the doors of the temple, one of which is partly open.[1]

The columns are fluted with composite capitals, between which is a screen or lattice of open marble work. To the left of the spectator is shown one column and a piece of the entablature of the Atrium.

The column is fluted and the capital is of a peculiar composite, differing from the conventional composite of the temple.

In the excavation of 1877 several fragments of fluted columns were found, and they are still, I believe, lying about half-way between the Temple of Vesta and that of Antoninus Pius.

They agree with the relief in their details as belonging to the temple. They are fluted with the flutes filled in their lower part ; cabled ; at the half-circle of the column there is a plain flange left unfluted, projecting one inch from the column, and 5 inches wide ; on the edges of the flange there are notches 20 inches apart. To this flange by means of the notches the marble cancellus or screen was fixed between the columns.

[1] *Gli edifize di Roma Antica*

There is evidence that this marble screen was destroyed in the ancient days, probably after the suppression of the worship in A.D. 392; and the temple being put to other uses, iron rails were placed between the columns, for the holes where the iron was fixed into the columns exist ; some of them with the lead setting remaining.

As the church authorities possessed the buildings of the Vestals, their temple may have been turned into a Christian church, as was the round Temple of Hercules in the Forum Boarium, and the iron rails would be placed between the columns, as they are there.

On one of the fragments of the columns the lower part of the flange has been reduced in height and the upper part fluted to agree with the rest of the column.

Amongst these remains is a peculiar composite capital differing from the one belonging to the Temple of Vesta, supporting the inscription of the Shrine of Mercury. The upper part has the Ionic volute below which is an egg and dot moulding, then upright flutings ; whilst beneath these is the usual acanthus leaf for the lower part.

Besides the three beautiful and well-preserved composite capitals of the Shrine of Mercury, there are three Corinthian capitals close by, which may have belonged to the Atrium Vestæ, but not to the Temple, where the columns were composite, as has been proved above.

There is also a piece of one of the engaged columns of the Regia, fluted and cabled, as represented on the relief ; the piece of marble from which this projects, is 5 inches high and 2 inches wide, and one of its ends has ornamental work showing that it was an end engraved column.

These capitals may have belonged to the Temple of Vesta. The relief shows composite capitals, not Corinthian. They are short like those at the Temple of Vesta at Tivoli.

A section of the Temple has now been restored with these remains.

THE ALTAR OF VESTA

UPON the steps of the Temple of Jupiter Victor on the Palatine Hill is a circular altar, placed there by Com. Rosa. It was found in the open space behind that temple, called the Area Palatina, in January, 1868. It is of white marble, 37½ in. in diameter, 27 in. high, standing on a travertine base 9 in. high, 41 in. in front and rear, and 40 in. on the sides ; and is inscribed as mentioned on p. 119, of which the translation is as follows :

> Gnæus Domitius Calvinus, son of Marcus,
> High Priest.
> Consul, the second time, General;
> Dedicated from the spoils of war.

Was it the altar of Mars or of Vesta ? (see p. 119 *et seq.*). On the whole, I incline to the latter.

Domitius Calvinus was consul for the second time with Asinius Pollio in 40 B.C. (Josephus, *A.J.*, XIV, 14; Dio Cassius, XLVIII, 15.) He was saluted " Imperator," or Victorious General, by his troops in Spain. (*Ib.* 42.)

A denarius bears his portrait with the word, OSCA, a town in Andalusia, and on the reverse, sacrificial instruments, with the inscription, DOM. COS. ITER. IMP., which agrees with the inscription on the altar.

Ten inches to the left of the last line is a piece of iron dowelled in with lead, a similar piece being at 8½ in. to the right of the end line. They are 37½ in. apart, front measurement.

To the left of the left piece, 14 in., and 6½ in. from

the top of the altar is a similar piece of iron run in with lead.

Above the moulding which encircles the base of the altar is a mark all round 4 in. deep, probably of a metal band.

On the top of the altar a circular cavity is cut, forming a basin 7 in. from the edge, 24 in. in diameter, 9 in. deep, having at the sides thirty-nine spiral grooves cut in the marble. At the bottom of this cavity is a rectangular depression 9 in. long, 6 in. wide, and $1\frac{1}{2}$ in. deep.

I believe that a bronze brazier fitted into this cavity, and that in it was kept burning the perpetual fire, and that it stood originally in the centre of the Temple of Vesta in the Forum Romanum. As that Temple was circular, so was the altar within it, as represented on the denarius of the Empress Julia Domna Pia, alluded to above, and agreeing with Ovid's statement, " No angle projects in it."

A denarius of the Antia Gens represents a circular altar with the flame burning on it, and on the obverse, an ox's head, similar to those at the Vicus ad Capita Bubula, between the Temples of Vesta and Castor.

We need not be surprised at this altar being found a long way from the Temple of Vesta, for it is by no means an uncommon thing in Rome to find objects at a considerable distance from their original sites.

In fact there existed in the Stadium on the Palatine Hill, yet further off, two pedestals that were removed from the Atrium Vestæ by Theodoric in A.D. 500. They were taken back to the Atrium in 1902.

We have the historical fact that Gnæus Domitius Calvinus, who commanded Cæsar's centre at the battle of Pharsalia, restored the Regia 38 B.C. (p. 102.)

Dion Cassius says :

" The gold which he received from the Spanish cities he used by expending some on his triumph, but the greater part in re-building the Regia which had been entirely consumed by fire.

He restored and dedicated it, splendidly decorating

it with, amongst other things, statues which he had borrowed from Augustus with the intention of returning ; but when Augustus asked for them, he replied, ' I have not servants enough to bring them to you, but you who have so many can send for them.' This, Augustus was afraid to do, lest he should be accused of sacrilege." (Dion Cassius, XLVIII, 42.)

The Regia adjoined the Temple of Vesta, and as it was rebuilt by Calvinus, it is probable that this altar was made at the same time for the Temple of Vesta. Its details, as we have pointed out, are unlike any other altar, although its circular form is not uncommon.

I know of only three instances when the fire went out through neglect :

(1) In 206 B.C. " The fire was extinguished through the neglect, during the night, of the Vestal, who was whipped with a scourge by order of the Pontifex Maximus, Publius Licinius." This has already been referred to in discussing the discipline of the Vestals. (Livy, XXVIII, 11.)

(2) Livy tell us briefly that in 179 B.C., "The sacred fire was extinguished (*Epit.*, XLI).

(3) In 190 B.C., when the fire apparently was extinguished, it was relighted on the appeal of the High Priestess Æmilia to the Goddess Vesta by the spontaneous ignition of a piece of the Vestal's linen garment when cast on the cold altar.

It is interesting to note that the garment in question, according to Valerius Maximus (I, 7), was the best she had.

Her invocation of divine aid on this occasion has been referred to previously (p. 67 *et seq.*).

In 82 B.C. Quintus Mutius Scævola, the High Priest, was murdered in the Temple of Vesta, and the fire was extinguished by his blood. (Florus, III, 21; Lucan, *Phars.*, II, 126 ; Livy, *Epit.*, LXXXVI ; Cicero, *de Orat.*, III, 3.)

Festus (106), when he is speaking of the fire, says:

" If at any time the fire of Vesta was utterly extinguished the Virgins were punished by the Pontiff by scourging. By whom pieces of wood of a favourable material were rubbed in a way so long that they took fire, the virgins carrying it in a bronze sieve to the temple."

A coin of Vespasian's represents the Temple of Vesta with a circular altar in the interior, and a Vestal standing behind it.

Some years ago in clearing out the fountain in the Atrium Vestæ a small triangular marble pedestal for a lamp was discovered. This is sculptured in relief on each side.

On one side is a tree and under it an altar upon which the fire is burning ; perhaps this represents the altar of Vesta. The next has a nude female figure standing with her back to the spectator ; her arms are stretched upwards and outwards, whilst she holds some oval object in her hands, towards which she is looking. Her mantle has fallen off her. On the third side is a candelabra.

THE OFFICIAL HOUSE OF THE VESTALS

(ATRIUM VESTÆ)

ADJOINING the Regia was the House of the Vestals, at first a humble primitive dwelling, at a later date a stately edifice with a spacious open court consonant with the dignity of the Vestal Virgins, and the high esteem in which they were held.

The centre of the group of buildings was the round Temple of Vesta, which has been described above.

Dionysius (II, 67) informs us that "the Vestals lived by the Temple of the goddess." Servius, commenting on Virgil's *Æneid*, 7, 153, says the Atrium Vestæ was at some distance from the Temple.

The east end of the Forum was enclosed by the three edifices, the Atrium Vestæ, the Temple of Vesta and the Regia of Numa. This agrees with the poetical notices and the actual remains ; the Regia being on the north, and the Atrium on the south side of the Temple.

To those who have studied the topography of the lower end of the Forum Romanum on the spot, it is well known that the passages in the classic writers, where the buildings belonging to the Vestal Virgins are spoken of, do not agree with the position of the Atrium Vestæ discovered some years ago ; and that edifice is not an atrium but a peristylium.

The lower, or east, end of the Forum at the present day is closed in with the Temple of Castor, the site of the arch of Fabius and the temple-tomb of Cæsar ; but before these edifices were erected, it was bounded by the buildings appertaining to the High Priest and the Vestal Virgins ; thus, the Atrium Vestæ, the Temple of Vesta, the Regia. The Temple stood in the centre ; on the right (north) was the official residence of the High Priest, and on the left (south) the home of the Vestals.

A careful examination of the remains at the east end of the Forum shows construction of the time of the kings—that is, blocks of tufa appertaining to the three different edifices. If anyone examines the podium of the Temple of Vesta, he will observe that the lower part of it is constructed with great blocks of tufa—the original construction of Numa—and that upon it is rough rubble work of the time of Septimus Severus— a necessary raising of the podium after the fire of Commodus, as the surrounding ground had been raised.

Beneath the brick-work chambers on the right (north) of the Temple may be seen tufa construction— part of the original Regia of Numa. On the left of the Temple only a small piece of tufa is now to be seen in situ—remains of the original Atrium Vestæ. The steps leading up and the door of the Temple are to the east, so that as the Vestal watched the fire by night her eyes might be gladdened by the first rays of dawn on the eastern horizon.

Dion Cassius (LIV, 27) informs us that the residence of the High Priest adjoined the Temple of Vesta, and that Augustus gave the Regia to the Vestals because it adjoined their buildings. This gift is alluded to by Ovid (*F.*, VI, 263) : " This place which sustains the Atrium Vestæ was then the great palace of the unshorn Numa."

Dionysius (II, 67) says the Vestals lived adjoining the Temple of the goddess ; in fact, the Temple was between the two residences.

Horace (*Odes*, I, 2, 13)[1] describes how the Tiber, receding from the right, or Etruscan bank, reaches the Forum, probably by the Cloaca Maxima, as has happened several times, and threatens destruction to the Regia and the Temple of Vesta.

He mentions the Regia first and the Temple next, going from left to right.

In his celebrated satire (I, 9), coming by chance

[1] See also p. 111.

down the Via Sacra, from the Palatine, he meets the bore, and one-fourth of the day was gone when they came " ad Vestæ " ; that is, to the buildings belonging to the Vestals—the Regia which abutted on to the Sacred Way.

Thus, in these two passages, he mentions both the edifices. Ovid (T., III, i, 27), in sending his book from the Argiletum, the book-sellers' quarter, makes the guide say, " This is the Forum of Cæsar," and as they pass through the Forum of Julius Cæsar, and strike the Via Sacra in the Forum Romanum, " The way which derives its name from the sacred rites." As they go along, he says, " This is the shrine of Vesta, which contains the Palladium and the eternal fire."

As the Palladium was kept in the Regia, he therefore hints at both edifices ; then he says, speaking of the Regia, " This was the little palace of the ancient Numa." Thus he speaks of both buildings, enumerating them from right to left. Proceeding up the hill, they turn to the right, at the church of St. Francesca, and enter the Palatine at the Porta Mugonia by the Temple of Jupiter Stator.

Martial (I, 70), in sending his book to Proculus, enumerates the buildings from left to right, in the reverse order to Ovid.

He commences to describe the route from the well-known Temple of Castor and Pollux in the Forum.

From there, by the Sacred Way, the book would pass, having on its right, as it turned to the left, the Temple of Vesta. (" Canæ Vestæ " must be translated not aged Vestæ, but hoary or snow white, signifying the costume of the Vestals.)

Then, turning to the right, the book would skirt the Regia and commence the ascent of the Sacred Way up the Velia ; having the Palatine on its right. In front on the summit of the ridge stood the colossus of Nero with its rayed head, where now stands the tower of St. Francesca. The book was not to delay in admiring the statue, but was to turn to the left by the street which here runs out of the Via Sacra, the Vicus Eros.

At the corner were evidently the wayside altars or shrines of Bacchus and Cybele.

Then on the left, just past the Portico of the Basilica of Constantine, was the house of Proculus, the ruins of which can still be seen.

The passage translates as follows :

" You ask the way ? I will tell you. In the vicinity of Castor
You will pass by snow white Vesta and the Virgins' house ;
Then by the Sacred Hill, you will direct your steps towards the venerable Palatine,
On which glisten many a statue of the all highest ruler.
Let not the wonderful radiated Colossus detain thee,
Whose grandeur delights in excelling the masterpiece of Rhodes,
Turn your steps here, where are the roofs of dripping Bacchus,
Where stands the dome of Cybele and the paintings of her priests.
Immediately on the left, in front, are the stately Penates and you must approach the Atrium of the lofty house."

This group of buildings belonging to the Vestals was destroyed in the terrible fire of A.D. 191 and when the restoration was made by Julia Domna, she built a new and larger residence for the Vestals, extending the home over part of the site of the house (belonging to the State) in which Cæsar had lived. This has been uncovered in the recent excavations. The new edifice was built as a peristylium, but the old name was retained, and this accounts for the anomaly of the present Atrium Vestæ being a peristylium.

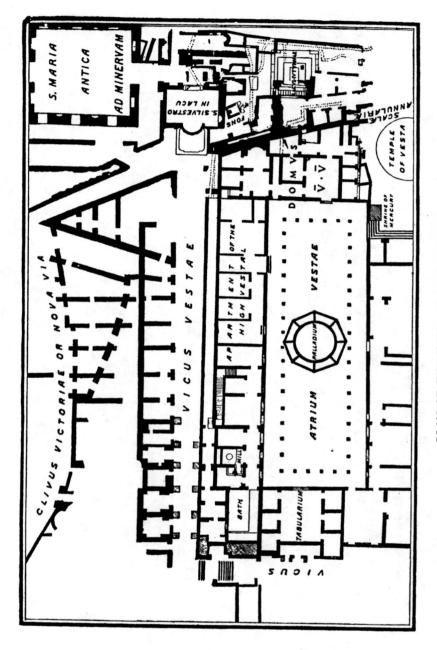

PLAN OF THE HOME OF THE VESTALS

(By permission of Dr. Forbes.)

THE PRIVATE HOME OF THE VESTALS

AFTER the destruction by fire in A.D. 192 the Atrium Vestæ and the Temple of Vesta were rebuilt by Julia Domna, the wife of the emperor Septimius Severus, and this inscription has been found in its vicinity :

VESTAE . DONVM . PRO . SALVTE .
IVLIAE . AVG . . MATRIS .
M. ANTONINI. AVG. N.P.M.
EVTYCHES . FICTOR . CVM . FILIS.
VOTO . SVSCEPTO .[1]

To commemorate this rebuilding, a silver coin was struck by the empress, bearing her head on the obverse (p. 129).

An extended site was selected for the new home, more under the Palatine, beyond their Temple, to the right from the Forum, and partly over the House of Cæsar, which had also been destroyed, east of the original Atrium.

A flight of six steps gave access into a large peristylium, 221 ft. long by 75 ft. wide, paved with a black mosaic.

Twelve feet out from the sides was the cloister, formed with 18 columns of cipollino marble on each side, and 6 at each end, counting the corner ones twice over.

The east end is paved with slabs of various coloured marbles ; the other end and sides with white mosaic.

At the west end was a communication with the old Atrium, rebuilt and incorporated into their residence. The side rooms were evidently offices of the household.

On the south side are a set of rooms, separated from

[1] Though the Empress is mentioned it is not possible to determine what particular offering is referred to.

the others, with remains of frescoes, marble walls and mosaic floors—evidently the rooms of the High Vestal connected with their religious duties.

At the east end, reached by a flight of four steps, is the Tablinum, or drawing-room, where they would receive their guests. Off this are six small chambers, evidently one for each Vestal in which to deposit those objects given into their sacred custody. On the left are other rooms, and on the right, bath chambers.

There was an upper cloister, of which three columns of breccia corallina marble exist, reached by a flight of stairs off each side of the peristylium.

Off this were the private rooms of the Vestals, into which no one was allowed to enter except their female domestics.

They show traces of mosaic floors and terra-cotta heating flues, also baths. Remains of a flight of stairs show that there was a third floor at this end.

Towards the east end of the open court is a tank for water, which was supplied by an aqueduct, one of the grids of which can be looked into about half-way down on the north side. This fountain has steps down into it for the convenience of drawing water for domestic purposes. The specus (culvert) goes on to the bath chambers. Three heads of Vestals, a head of Minerva, some lamps, a black marble weight, the pedestal above described, and some coins were found in it.

In the centre is a circular foundation from which walls radiate, forming an octagonal border. It would appear that on this border was a railing, and that on the circular part stood the shrine of Ops Consiva possibly containing the Palladium, etc., when the Regia was abandoned.

From the east end of the south cloister a door gives access to a corridor, off which are the bath chambers, and the mill-room where the salt was ground, which the Vestals had to supply at the sacrifices. Parts of the mill exist, similar to those used for corn. Perhaps this was used for both purposes.

Horace (*O.*, III, 23, 20) speaks of :

"Holy spelt and leaping salt."

And Pliny says (*N.H.*, XXI, 89):

"It is in our sacred rites more particularly that the high importance of salt is to be recognised ; no offering ever being made unaccompanied by salt."

A relief on a pedestal in the Forum near the Arch of Severus shows one of the Vestals with the box of salt attending a sacrifice.

On the north side of the Vestals' residence is the Porticus Margaritaia ; on the south, the Vicus Vestæ ; at the east end, a street connects these two, the name of which we do not know. At the west end it is bounded by the Scalæ Anulariæ. (Suetonius, *Augustus*, 72.)

The following inscription was found in the Atrium, but removed :

PRO. SALVTE. DOMINI
NOSTRI. IMPERATOR
SEVERI. ALEXANDRI. PII
AVGVSTI. ET
IVLIAE. MAESAE. ET
IVLIAE. AVITAE
MAMEAE. SANCTISSIMARVM
AVGVSTARVM
GENIO. SANCTO. CASTROR.
PEREGRINORVM
T. FLAVIVS. DOMITIANVS
DOMO. NICOMEDIA. QUOD
SPECVLATOR.LEG.III.PARTH.
SEVERIANAE. VOVIT. HAS
TATVS. LEG. X. FRETENSIS
PRINCFPS. PEREGRINORVM
REDDEDIT.

For the weal of our Lord Emperor, Severus Alexander Pius Augustus, and of the most holy Augustæ Julia Mæsa and Julia Avita Mammæa, Titus Flavius Domitianus of Nicomedian birth now being hastatus (a second-class centurion) in the Tenth (Fretensis) legion and *princeps peregrinorum* (that is commandant of the Foreign Camp) has paid to the holy genius of the Foreign Camp, the offering which he vowed when he was speculator (orderly) of the Third Parthica Severiana Legion.

This gives the names of the grandmother, Julia Mæsa, and Julia Avita Mammæa, mother, of the emperor Alexander Severus. The house of Gaius Julius Avitus, the father of Mammea was found in 1879 in building the Costanzi theatre. The camp of the Foreign corps was on the Cœlian hill. They formed the guard of the Palatine.

According to a quaint incident mentioned by Plutarch, it would appear that a Vestal Virgin might own her own garden :

" For women, he (Crassus) lived as continent a life, as any Roman of his time : notwithstanding, afterwards being of riper years, he was accused by Plotinus to have deflowered one of the Vestall Nunnes called Licinia. But in troth the cause of that suspicion grew thus : Licinia had a goodly pleasaunt garden hard by the suburbs of the City wherewith Crassus was marvelously in love, and would faine have had it good chepe ; and upon this only occasion was often seene in speche with her, which made the people suspect him. But forasmuch it seemed to the judges that his covetousness was the cause that made him follow her, he was clered the incest suspected, but he never left following of the Nunne till he had got the garden of her." (*Crassus*, trans. by North.)

THE STREET OF VESTA

(VICUS VESTÆ)

AS far as I know, the Vicus Vestæ (the Street of Vesta) is not mentioned by name by any classical author, but it seems to have been the boundary between the 8th Forum region and the 10th Palatine region.

This street was discovered during the 1882 excavations running on a ledge of the Palatine, from the Vicus Tuscus, to the Via Sacra, to the right of the Arch of Titus ; and separating the present Atrium Vestæ from the Palace of Caligula and Hadrian.

Some writers call this street the Via Nova, but that followed another line altogether and was higher up on the Palatine. The Basis Capitolina which dates A.D. 136 mentions six streets in the 10th region, the Palatine, but does not mention the Vicus Vestæ. However, it is mentioned in an inscription found at the church of St. Paul's outside the walls, in July, 1878 (C.I.L., 30960) :

LARIBVS . AVG . ET . GENIO

IMP. CAES. M. AVRELI. SEVERI. ALEXANDRI

PII. FELICIS. AVG. PONT. MAX. TRIB. POT.II COS. PP

AEDICVLAM. REG. VIII. VICO. VESTAE. VETVSTATE
CONLAPSAM

A. SOLO. PECVNIA. SVA. RESTITVERVNT. MAGISTRI.
ANNI. DCCCCLXXVI

NIVS. PIVS. L. CALPVRNIVS. FELIX

C. IVLIVS. PATERNVS. PRAEF. VIGILVM

L. MARIO. MAXIMO II. L. ROSCIO. AELIANO. COS

CVRANTIBVS. M SERVILIO. CRISPO. ET. M. SERVILIO.

" To the august household gods and tutelar deity of the Emperor Cæsar, Marcus Aurelius Severus Alexander, holy, victorious, august, Chief Pontiff, for the second time with tribunician power, consul, Father of his Country, the Overseers for the year 976 (A.U.C.) (Anto)nius Pius, L. Calpurnius Felix, C. Julius Paternus Chief of Police, with their own money restored from the ground up, this shrine in the Eighth Region in the street of Vesta, which had fallen from old age, in the Consulship of L. Marius Maximus (for the second time) and L. Roscius Aelianus, the contractors being M. Servilius Crispus and M. Servilius."

From the inscription and consuls mentioned we learn that in the year A.D. 223 a shrine on the Vicus Vestæ, in the 8th region, was restored by the Magistri in the reign of the emperor Alexander Severus.

This restoration was probably made after the earthquake, when the whole street seems to have been restored.

The street is spanned by a series of arches, which have a very picturesque effect.

The construction shows that these arches were erected later than the walls and shops on either side, in fact, they were put in as flying buttresses to keep up the edifices on either side.

On the right of this street, in going towards the arch of Titus, from about the old Farnese entry to where it ran into the Via Sacra stood the celebrated house of Scaurus spoken of by Cicero and Pliny ; the exact position of which is described in detail by Asconius (in Cicero, *pro Scauro*, 23). He says :

" The house is in that part of the Palatine which is reached as one descends the Via Sacra and takes the first street (Vicus) on the left." The first street running out of the Via Sacra, as one comes down it from the Aedes Larum, is on the left and is the street in question, the Vicus Vestæ.

The passage in Asconius alone is sufficient to upset any theory about it being the Via Nova, for if it is the Via Nova, Asconius would have said " per proximam

Viam " and not " per proximum *vicum*." Vicus means a street in a town. Via means a road outside the city. The Via Sacra and the New Way were outside Roma Quadrata, so they were properly roads and not streets, and if the Via Nova was the first road going out of the Via Sacra on the left as one came down from the commencement of the Via Sacra, at the Aedes Larum on the Palatine, Asconius would have said "road," not "street."

VESTA'S DUST-BIN

IN some diggings made about the podium of the Temple of Vesta in the Forum, to the right of the entry a pit was found 3 ft. by 34 in. square and 6 ft. 9 in. deep, lined with peperino stone.

This is doubtless the ash-pit where the ashes from the altar were despatched and the sweepings of the temple ; which pit was cleared out once a year and the rubbish thrown away on the 15th of June.

" This is the day on which thou, O Tiber, dost roll to the deep, along thy Etrurian streams, the cleansings of the shrine of Vesta." (Ovid, *Fasti*, 6, 713.)

Festus says (344) :

" Stercus ex æde Vestæ XVII Kalendas Iulias defertur in angiportum medium fere clivi Capitolini, qui locus clauditur porta Stercoraria tantæ sanctitatis, maiores vestri esse iudicaverunt."

Varro, says (*L.L.*, VI, 32) :

" Dies qui vocatur, Quando Stercus Delatum, Fas : ab eo appellatus, quod eo die ex æde Vestæ stercus everritur, et per Capitolinum clivum in locum defertur certum."

The ashes seem to have been taken from the temple of Vesta to a trap-door (Porta Stercoraria), near the temple of Saturn, communicating with a drain, hence they went into the Cloaca Maxima, and so on into the Tiber.

Thus speaks the wife of the Flamen Dialis :

" Until the gently flowing Tiber shall have borne on his tawny waters, to the deep, the cleansings from the shrine of Ilian Vesta, I may not comb my cropped hair with my comb of boxwood, cut my nails with my knife, nor touch my husband, though he is the Priest of Jupiter, though he has been given to me by an eternal pact."[1]   (Ovid, *Fasti*, VI, 227 *et seq.*)

Varro (see above) and Festus both say that the refuse was taken to a place on the ascent to the Capitol ; Festus informing us that it was called the Porta Stercoraria.   Ovid twice says the refuse went into the Tiber.

Now, as the Clivus (or Capitoline Hill) is a long way from the Tiber, it could only have reached the river by means of the drain that runs under the Clivus.   We might mention that under the new road there is an opening (closed with a trap) which communicates with the drain.   The fact that the ashes were thrown away near the Temple of Saturn may have some connection with agriculture.   A tufa drain of the time of the kings was found in 1899 in front of the Temple of Saturn.

[1] i.e. by the confarreate marriage which did not allow divorce.

THE WATER JAR (FUTILE) OF THE VESTALS

THERE was a curious prohibition in carrying out the ceremonies connected with the Sacred Rites that the vessel holding water must not be placed on the ground. In sprinkling and purifying the shrine each morning with water it was an institution of Numa that the water must be drawn from a particular fountain near to the Regia, although at a later date it was lawful to use any water from a spring or running stream, but not any water passing through pipes.

To obviate any danger of this law being broken, a special receptacle was used.

This was the "futile," a vessel shaped like an inverted cone, and therefore incapable of standing by itself.

Servius thus describes it :

" A futile is a sort of vase with a wide mouth and a narrow bottom, which they were accustomed to use in the rites of Vesta, because water drawn for the rites of Vesta is not stood on the ground ; if this is done it is an offence. For this reason the vase was designed, such that it could not stand, but when put down it was at once upset."[1]

" Futile vas quoddam est lato ore, fundo angusto, quo utebantur in sacris Vestæ, quia aqua ad sacra hausta in terra non ponitur, quod si fiat piaculum est. unde excogitatum vas est, quod stare non posset, sed positum statim effunderetur." (Servius, on *Aeneid*, XI, 339.)

It is worthy of note that simplicity was the keynote of all the sacred vessels used in the rites of Vesta, even

[1] For this reason a man who let out secrets was called " Futilis."

at a time when vessels of silver and gold were elsewhere common in Rome.

The Vestals always presented their offering in
primitive vessels of earthenware, a memory of the
simple origin of the Faith.   Their utensils were known
as " Numa's Pottery."   Specimens of this antique
pottery were discovered in recent years in the Temple
of Vesta, and in the House of the Vestals.

VESTA'S GROVE

THE old grove of Vesta which once skirted the foot of the Palatine Hill on the side of the Forum was probably an oak grove, for an oak appears growing beside the Temple of Vesta in the relief to be seen in a gallery of the Uffizi at Florence.

In recent years charred embers of the Sacred Vestal fire were discovered in the Forum, an analysis of which proved them to have been from the pith of oak branches.

Under the Aventine, according to Ovid (*Fasti*, III, 295), was a grove of evergreen oaks which appears to have been no other than the grove of Egeria[1] outside the Porta Capena.

Livy (I, 21) translated by Philemon Holland describes the Grove of Egeria as follows :

" Furthermore there was a grove, the widest whereof was watred continually by a spring that issued out of a darke and shaddowed cave, into which, because Numa used oft to retire himselfe alone, without any other, as it were to have familiar companie with Aegeria, hee dedicated that grove unto the Muses, for that, their assistance also in counsell and advise hee desired together with his wife Aegeria. And to Faith alone he instituted a solenne yearely festivall day, and erected a chappell, Unto which he commanded the Flamines to ride in an arched or embowed close chariot, drawn with two horses, and to sacrifice and execute their function, with their hands covered and wrapped close to their fingers ends, signifying thereby, that faith is to be kept and preserved, and that her seat was sacred and consecrated even upon the right hands. Many other sacrifices and places for sacrifices that the priests call Argeos, did he appoint and dedicate."

---

[1] Modern archæologists, however, differ as to the site of the grove.

SILVER COIN STRUCK BY THE
EMPRESS JULIA DOMNA TO COM-
MEMORATE THE RE-BUILDING OF
THE ATRIUM VESTAE AFTER THE
FIRE OF A.D. 191. ON THE REVERSE
AS SHOWN ABOVE IS THE TEMPLE
OF VESTA WITH SIX VIRGINS, TWO
OF WHOM ARE COMBINING IN AN
OBLATION

CONCLUSION

IN the preceding pages I have endeavoured to portray the distinguished place which the Vestal Virgins, the priestesses of Holy Mother Vesta, occupied in the life of Rome, primitive, regal, republican and imperial.

It is significant of the hold which their cult obtained over the religious life of Rome that their functions remained unchanged and their importance increased rather than diminished, in spite of the many political upheavals in the evolution of the Roman people.

Nothing less than a complete revolution in religious thought, and the advent of a greater Faith, was powerful enough to destroy the worship that had defied the chances and changes of a thousand years.

We observe its beginnings in the dim ages of myth and mystery, when the miracle of Fire, with its powers for good and evil, first became known to men.

It was to them a thing of wonder, supernatural in its origin to the primitive mind, and therefore meet to be guarded and even worshipped, a task which could only be entrusted to the purest and most exalted, the virgin daughters of Kings.

And so the fire, and the hearth on which it was kindled and kept alive, became the centre of family worship, with its virgin priestesses as guardians of the sacred flame whose brides they were in mystic spiritual union.

Through all the phases of Rome's evolution, from the early hamlet to the Eternal City, the sacredness of the family hearth remained the foundation of Roman religious feeling, symbolised by the little Temple of

Mother Vesta, the mysterious goddess of whom no statue was ever made.[1]

In spite of the changes in political life, in spite of the opulence and magnificence of the palmy days of Rome, the cult of Vesta stood unchanging for a thousand years, the symbol of the ancient Numa's simple faith, of which the only relics left to us to-day are the broken statues of her ancient priestesses and the remnants of their dwelling-place, mute but noble reminders of a glory that is departed.

---

[1] Ovid (*Fasti*, VI, 295) tells us that he had been stupid enough to believe that there was a statue of Vesta in the Ædes Vestæ, but discovered his mistake.

"Esse diu stultus Vestæ simulacra putavi;
Mox didici curvo nulla subesse tholo."

APPENDIX I (Note to p. 33.)

Cicero (*Phil.*, II, 84.)

" Sed ne forte ex multis rebus gestis M. Antoni rem unam pulcherrimam transiliat oratio, ad Lupercalia veniamus. Non dissimulat, patres conscripti ; apparet esse commotum, sudat, pallet.

Quidlibet, modo non nauseet, faciat, quod in porticu Minucio fecit.

Quæ potest esse turpitudinis tantæ defensio ? Cupio audire, ut videam ubi rhetoris sit tanta merces. Sedebat in rostris collega tuus, amictus toga purpurea, in sella aurea, coronatus."

Then occurs the offer of the crown to Cæsar.

(*Ib.*, III, 12.) " Nec vero M. Antonium consulem post Lupercalia debuistis putare ; quo enim ille die, populo Romano inspectante, nudus unctus ebrius est contionatus et id egit, ut collegæ diadema imponeret. Eo die se non modo consulatu, sed etiam libertate abdicavit."

APPENDIX II (Note to p. 70.)

" Sacerdotum et numerum et dignitatem sed et commoda auxit præcipue Vestalium virginum. Quumque in demortuæ locum aliam capi oporteret, ambirentque multi, ne filias in sortem darent ; adiuravit, si cuiusquam neptium suarum competeret ætas, oblaturum se fuisse eam. Etiam ex antiquis cærimoniis, paulatim abolita, restituit ; et salutis augurium Diali Flamini sacrum Lupercale, ludos seculares et compitalicios. Lupercalibus vetuit currere imberbes." (Suetonius, *Augustus*, XXXI.)

APPENDIX III   (Note to p. 73.)

Heliogabalus and the Palladium. (Lampridius, *Helio.*, III–VI.)

Sed ubi primum ingressus est urbem, omissis iis quæ in provincia gerebantur, Heliogabalum in Palatino monte iuxta ædes imperatorias consecravit eique templum fecit, studens et Matris typum et Vestæ ignem, et Palladium et ancilia et omnia Romanis veneranda in illud transferre templum et id agens ne quis Romæ deus nisi Heliogabalus coleretur. . . .

In virginem Vestalem incestum admisit. Sacra Populi Romani sublatis penetralibus profanavit. Ignem perpetuum exstinguere voluit, nec Romanas tantum exstinguere religiones voluit, sed per orbem terræ unum studens ut Heliogabalus deus unus ubique coleretur ; et in penum Vestæ, quod solæ virgines solique pontifices adeunt, irrupit pollutus ipse omni contagione morum cum iis qui se polluerant. Et penetrale sacrum est auferre conatus ; quumque seriam quasi veram rapuisset, quamvis virgo maxima falsam monstravit atque in ea nihil reperisset, applosam fregit ; nec tamen quicquam religioni dempsit, quia plures similes factæ dicuntur esse, ne quis veram unquam possit auferre. Hæc quum ita essent, signum tamen quod Palladium esse credebat abstulit ; et auro fictum in sui dei templum locavit.

INDEX